WORD PLAY
WORD POWER

WORD PLAY WORD POWER

■

A WOMAN'S PERSONAL GROWTH WORKBOOK

■

BY KIMBERLEY SNOW

Conari Press
Berkeley, California

Printed in the United States of America

Cover by Joan Edwards

Illustrations by Margaret Mason

ISBN: 0-943233-04-6

For my daughters,
with love

ACKNOWLEDGMENTS

The author would like to thank the following for permission to reprint the works indicated:

Excerpt from WOMEN OF WISDOM by Tsultrim Allione. Copyright © 1986 by Tsultrim Allione. Reprinted by permission of Associated Book Publishers (U.K.) LTD.

"DAILY COURAGE DOESN'T COUNT" from I AM NOT A PRACTICING ANGEL by alta. Copyright © 1975 by alta. Reprinted by permission of the author.

"SONG FOR A GIRL ON HER FIRST MENSTRUATION" by Anonymous, translation by Joe Prentuo, from THE OTHER VOICE: 20TH Century Women's Poetry in Translation, ed. Joanna Bankier, et al. Copyright © 1976. Reprinted by permission of Joanna Bankier.

Excerpt from SURFACING by Margaret Atwood. Copyright © 1972. Reprinted by permission of SIMON & SCHUSTER, INC.

Excerpt from MEMOIRS OF A DUTIFUL DAUGHTER by Simone de Beauvoir. Copyright © 1958 by Librairie Gallimard. Reprinted by permission of Harper & Row Publishers, Inc.

Excerpt from COMBAT IN THE EROGENOUS ZONE by Ingrid Bengis. Copyright © 1972 by Ingrid Bengis. Reprinted by permission of The Wendy Weil Agency, Inc.

Excerpt from AMONG WOMEN by Louise Bernikow. Copyright © 1980. Reprinted by permission of Crown Publishers Inc.

Excerpt from THE KIN OF ATA ARE WAITING FOR YOU by Dorothy Bryant. Copyright ©1971 by D.M. Bryant. Reprinted by permission of Random House, Inc.

"The Kiwi Bird" by Nina Cassian from LADY OF MIRACLES, Poems by Nina Cassian, Selected and Translated from the Romanian by Laura Schiff. Copyright © 1982, Cloud Marauder Press, 1922 Stuart St., Berkeley, CA 94703. Reprinted by permission of Laura Schiff.

Excerpt from HOME BEFORE DARK by Susan Cheever. Copyright © 1984 by Susan Cheever. Reprinted by permission of Houghton Mifflin Company.

Excerpt from WITH CHILD: A DIARY OF MOTHERHOOD by Phyllis Chesler. Copyright © 1979 by Phyllis Chesler. Reprinted by permission of the author.

Excerpt totalling 3 pages from WOMANSPIRIT RISING by Carol P. Christ and Judith Plaskow. Copyright © 1979 by Carol P. Christ and Judith Plaskow. Reprinted by permission of Harper & Row, Publishers, Inc.

"Hips," first published in THE HOUSE ON MANGO STREET by Sandra Cisneros (2nd ed., Houston: Arte Publico Press—University of Houston, 1988). Reprinted by permission of Arte Publico Press.

Excerpt from SISTER AGE by M.F.K. Fisher. Copyright © 1964, 1983 by M.F.K. Fisher. Reprinted by permission of Alfred A. Knopf, Inc.

Excerpt from THE SECOND STAGE by Betty Friedan. Copyright © 1981, reprinted by permission of SIMON & SCHUSTER, INC.

Excerpt from THE TRAFFIC IN WOMEN AND OTHER ESSAYS ON FEMINISM, pp. 37-38 by Emma Goldman. Copyright © 1970. Reprinted by permission of Times Change Press, Box 1380, Ojai, CA 93023.

CONTENTS

SECTION THREE: UTILIZING YOUR WRITING

INTRODUCTION

"I started writing because of a terrible feeling of powerlessness: I felt I was drifting and obscure, and I rebelled against that. I didn't see what I could do to change my condition. I wanted to control rather than be controlled, to ordain rather than be ordained, and to relegate rather than be relegated."

Anita Brookner

Since I taught my first women's studies class in 1969, I have been a witness to and a participant in a great wave of change as new and often astonishing forms of self-definition for women came into being. At times I felt enormous exhilaration riding the crest of this wave; at other times it seemed as if the wave had crashed on top of me. One thing that kept me afloat through two decades of dramatic change—that still helps me keep my head above water—is writing: making sense of the incredible chaos of choices through the discipline of self articulation. I remember one particularly bad period when, as a graduate student and single mother, I felt almost destroyed by my own feminist determination to "have it all." I remember saying to myself: "I feel like one of the eggs that got broken to make the feminist omelette." Then I thought, "Hey, that's not bad." So I wrote it down and as I did so, other words followed, words that led to release and a renewed sense of direction.

Through the play of our imagination, we gain the power to expand our limits, to integrate change and to guide our personal growth. Writing releases us into a timeless world where all things are possible. In this magical realm, we can reclaim past events, retrieve former selves, live out what almost was, what could have been. Through writing and visualization we are able to develop a personal language that fills out the hollows and blank spaces in our lives, to make sense of and give reality to our experience. In this private arena where conscious and unconscious meet and interact, we are granted a unique opportunity to negotiate peace settlements between inner and outer, between self and other.

WORD PLAY/WORD POWER grew directly out of writing and women's studies courses I've taught over the years. Most of the readings in this book deal with contemporary issues and ideas about women; the writing and visualization exercises, which came out of the readings, are designed to turn you into an active participant. To think and to write about women's issues is to engage actively in the process of confronting, integrating, and personalizing the enormous changes in our lives, hopes, and possibilities.

Literature is one of the means we have always used to gain consciousness of our situation, to grapple with change, and to imagine a different kind of future. In the past two decades the feminine side of our culture has developed its own literary voice, reporting experiences previously excluded from what had been defined and taught as literature. Feminism made us realize that our perceptions count, and that we must choose our own words for naming, our own methods for expression. The new women writers are you and me, Adrienne Rich and the waitress who spends an hour with her journal each night. For underlying the words of published writers has run the undersound of women writing to themselves. If we see literature as the expression of a generation, speaking to itself, then I think it fair to say the essential literary voice of this period could be heard in our journals.

Countless changes, large and small, have been facilitated and helped by journal and personal writing in ways that are not obvious, and can't be measured in terms of book sales or bestseller lists. Incalculable individual adjustments have been worked through in the steady outpouring of women's words into their notebooks and journals, words often trying to make sense of lives their writers never expected to lead.

This book emerged out of a need felt by many people I encountered in classes and workshops to expand their journal work into an more structured relationship with writing, to make writing a living and active part of their personal lives. By letting their writing be guided by exercises and suggestions, they found that they were released from a sense of personal limitation, were nudged into saying something exciting, creative, original, and understood something new about themselves in the process.

One of my most abiding pleasures as a writing teacher has been to watch the joy and amazement of a student who has been surprised into writing at a level she didn't think possible. As anyone who has ever kept a journal knows, you don't have to be interested in becoming a professional author to enjoy and profit from putting things down on paper. There is—dare I say it?—too much stress today on publishing, too much emphasis on the product of writing, too little on the process.

What I have found is that the value of writing, the sense of connection, comes not at the point a play of mine is produced or an article published, but in the primary process of creation. When I'm writing hard, a sort of humming starts at the edge of my consciousness: earth slides away, the sky opens. I'm in, quite literally, another world. Something comes to me, through me, something sings me, hums me. Each and every one of us can participate in this primary creative act, can connect with this source.

Over the years I found that it is easy to read coolly, superficially, only with the mind, but writing is different. Writing requires emotional involvement, it engages the whole self. By simply picking up a pen and writing for 20 minutes on a given subject, we often find out not only what we think about a topic, but also what we feel, what we fear, and what we hope. To cast material into a play, poem, or short story will frequently reveal hidden truths and latent ideas in a way that nothing else can.

However, if you are uncomfortable with the idea of writing your thoughts down, you can still use this book. When the exercises say write, using the visualization technique described on page 17. Perhaps, after doing some of the exercises as visualizations, you will feel ready to begin to write. Either way, the exercises in this book have proven to be capable of provoking a thoughtful response. A large number and wide variety of suggestions are presented to allow you to pick and choose among them. The exercises are designed to provoke, to tease, to challenge, and to clarify views and feelings. Some may help you to let off steam, examine personal situations, or assist in the working through of problems. Others are designed to strengthen your writing ability.

Certain of the exercises are very general; others, very specific. I've found that providing a mix of options for people is the best way to facilitate personal creativity. I encourage you to experiment with the exercises that appear to have little to do with your background or might seem foreign to your experience. Through working with the imagination, we can slip the moorings of our own personality to look at the world through another's eyes, to walk in his or her shoes. By imagining someone else's situation, we develop understanding and compassion, explore new ideas, new modes of being.

The book is divided into three sections: WRITING ABOUT WRITING, WRITING ABOUT WOMEN, and UTILIZING YOUR WRITING. The first contains readings and exercises designed to get you comfortable with the writing process. The second section's readings reflect the major topics that have absorbed women writers—love, marriage, work, divorce, sexuality, children, aging, dying—often with new twists and insights designed to jar you into unexplored territory. Some of the readings, Perera's piece on the animus-ego, for instance, may introduce a subject for the first time. Others, such as statistics on women in the work force, represent a reminder—almost in shorthand—that here's a matter we still need to think about, one as yet unresolved, but over-articulated. Like so many individual journeys, the selections here begin with the personal, move through the political and social, then on to the spiritual.

The final section, UTILIZING YOUR WRITING, offers a series of readings and exercises to facilitate the integration of writing into your life—whether that is in terms of personal growth or publication. Here you'll find readings and exercises on marketing your work, polishing for publication, and how to use your journal to better understand your major life issues.

In short, the readings and exercises in WORD PLAY/WORD POWER provide a technique for you to confront and incorporate some of the dramatic changes of the past two decades and to help you discover your relationship to writing itself. Hopefully, this book will provide you with a way of better understanding yourself and give you new tools for self-help and healing as well as enhance your ability to express yourself in words. In class or out, the readings and exercises are designed to help you sort and integrate the conflicting demands made upon women today. Most importantly, through the imagining of a different or better future, these exercises and readings will help to turn that vision into a reality.

USING THIS BOOK

VISUALIZATION

If you don't wish to write, skip Section One and go straight to Section Two. Use your own method of visualization or try this one:

Quiet your mind by concentrating on your breathing, a fine stream of air going in and out, in and out. Read the exercises. Don't think. If a thought does pass by, just let it think itself, without having to pay much attention to it. Like a child watching television.

If obsessive thoughts keep popping to the surface of your mind like boiling soup, you might want to stop and take a vigorous 20 minute walk to work on these specific thoughts so you can return and go deeper into the visualization.

One way or another, wait until your mind clears, until it functions as a reasonably still pool out of which images spontaneously appear. Then read the exercise again.

Let your imagination take over as in a daydream. At first, you may need to nudge the characters into motion or to guide the action. If your mind is very scattered, just keep returning to the central image of the exercise until you are able to hold it steady. For instance, if the exercise is to visualize someone you love, you might find it helps to "build" an image by concentrating on a number of specific details about the person in turn (color of hair, the way it falls over the forehead; laugh lines around the mouth, her habit of bunching up her shoulders; etc.). Once you've centered your mind on the visual image you've constructed, other aspects about the person—such as her emotional effect on you will follow. In time, you'll learn how to simultaneously control and not-control the visualization, how to allow for play while still concentrating.

Visualization gets easier with practice. You can do it anywhere: standing at the sink, on a bus. Don't worry whether you have technicolor visions, that isn't what visualization is all about. If you can dream (and we all do every single night) you can form visual images; but sometimes in visualization, you may receive an emotional "state" rather than a moving picture. Others find they get images like photographs at the time of an emotional release; some experience a video of the event when it's over.

Still others, like me, work it out in writing. But it is all using the imagination to improve the quality and clarity of your own life.

Even non-writers might want to do the CLUSTERING and BIG PICTURE exercises in Section Three. If you do, except for the initial notes to yourself, simply substitute a good think for "write." Or you might want to combine visualization with writing exercises in your own way.

Learn your own pattern. Experiment to see what works best for you in visualizing the exercises which lead to your personal change, integration, and growth.

WRITING

It's a common recognition that the process of writing is uncomfortable or even torturous for many people, particularly those whose desire to write is especially intense. But this primary, easily accessible, cheap, and non-caloric way of getting in touch with ourselves and with others should not be shut off out of fear. I have found that even the most tightly clutched fear can be relaxed, and I have included several different exercises designed to lessen anxiety in writing and to bypass or silence the harsh inner judge. This book begins with them, along with student samples. After completing this sequence, even the unsure writer should be more comfortable with the act of writing.

Many writers find that if they warm up by simply writing whatever comes into their head, their "real" writing project goes much better. May Sarton advised that you get up in the morning and go straight to the typewriter while the "gates to the unconscious are still open."

In writing classes, they call this pre-writing or free writing, but whatever it's called it works the same way, i.e., to get the brain into its holistic mode. The exercises in this book are designed to do this in a more structured way, to keep the holistic approach; but rather than have to formulate questions as well as answers, you are asked to write on the questions asked by other women as they grappled with the same problems.

Other than the beginning sequence on "WRITING ABOUT WRITING," which should be completed first if you feel anxious about the writing process itself, there is no need to follow the exercises in the order they are presented here. The readings and the exercises range widely, so naturally some will appeal more than others. Some exercises you may want to do more than once, some not at all. Some you may wish only to think about.

When the exercise says "Write," this means for 20 minutes without stopping. (A kitchen timer is helpful.) Do not edit as you go along. Forget grammar, forget style, forget everything but the subject you are dealing with.

Be honest when you write, don't pose, don't write for an unseen audience of cheering fans or a panel of critical judges. Write for yourself, make language your own. In time, this will develop your own way of saying things, your own natural style. Simply concentrate on the subject at hand.

Many people feel very self conscious at first when they write. There is no way around this but to keep writing. Setting a clock and keeping the pen moving across the page also helps. If you find that you get absolutely stuck, go back and read what you have written so far, then try to reenter the process. Some say it is helpful to rewrite the word you can't get past over and over until the pen takes off.

If you are writing on a new topic or one that has so many parts you don't know where to start, it may be helpful to go through the process known as "clustering," described in the section "WRITING ABOUT WRITING." Often times, however, it is satisfying to use writing itself as a means of discovery. Remember, no one is watching. It doesn't matter whether you say what you mean at first or after a dozen pages.

If you stop and try to correct and polish as you go, the editing side of the brain may interfere with the creative side. The flow of ideas and images can falter and stop, dried up by rules and regulations. It's much better simply to let yourself go, to learn to write without inhibitions and without stopping. Sometimes I find that I'm writing in a voice that I don't like, a voice that sounds stuffy, or whiny, or prissy—whatever. I discovered that if I let that voice have its say, I can write beyond it to something else, but if I try to block it, I can't write anything at all. In later drafts, I simply cut the lines "she" wrote, that ninth-grade little twit who still survives somewhere in my head. My own method is to write through all the voices that insist on speaking up, to write and write until something else takes over, something larger than personal ego.

Once when asked how she knew when to stop working on a piece, Sandra Cisneros said, "When something surprises me, when I've learned something I didn't know before, then I know that I've reached the heart of that particular piece of writing." So, write for the surprise turn of event in the story or poem, the unexpected twist in the essay, the unanticipated revelation.

When the exercise asks you to write a play, don't say to yourself, "I don't know how to write a play. I've never written anything but a letter." The exercise isn't to write a play that is going to Broadway next week, but to use a form in which there is a more or less fixed setting and lots of dialogue. It can be three pages long and boring as a bowl of cold oatmeal, but forcing yourself to put everything you want to say into dialogue rather than description will develop your capacities in many different ways. Your next try at a play might be four pages long and be more like warm oatmeal with raisins. One thing you can be sure of, however, is that the next play you see or read will be much more vivid and interesting to you after your active participation in the form.

The same is true if the exercise asks you to write a short story. If you've read a short story, you know something of the form. Read more short stories and pay attention to how the writer works, what details are included to make the characters seem real, how background is used. Become the characters, feel the atmosphere, speak with their tongues, hear with their ears. Experiment.

Many people are afraid of poetry. "You want ME to write a poem?!" a student will say to me in horror. "Me? You don't understand, I'm a Business major. With a minor in Computer Science. You can't mean me." If you've never written a poem, imitate the style of the poet in the exercise if you wish. Don't try to write in rhyme. Do try to use language in an interesting or unusual way. Read a poem over and over to attempt to get inside of it. Fake it until you get the feeling of being what Robert Frost calls "poem possessed." If it still feels uncomfortable, try the exercise "GETTING STARTED ON A POEM" which presents a method for how to go about writing in this potentially intimidating form.

One of the biggest and most widespread misconceptions about writing is that "good" writers are somehow able to write complete, finished, polished prose in the first draft. That's like thinking that you can serve a multi-course dinner to 12 people without messing up the kitchen. While the stress in this book is not on editing, polishing, or publishing, it is a good idea to keep in mind that every professional writer goes through a lengthy process in writing. A professor once told me that to write a ten page paper, I should write 100 pages, then throw away the first 90. He didn't smile as he said it, either.

Don't ever feel guilty because of what you have written or how you have written it. Don't feel guilty if you haven't written at all. With professional writers, time away from a project can be as important as time at the typewriter. Agatha Christie claimed that the best time to plan a new book was when doing the dishes. The novelist Harriet Dooer used to garden when she was trying to work out a problem in her writing, attacking the crab grass with vigor. I sew. During an especially long writing project, I seem to need to finish something tangible, to have a physical product. Perhaps it would be a good idea to get a special notebook or binder to use for these exercises. Be sure and leave several blank pages at the end of a 20 minute exercise so you can go back and add to it another time. A workshop member once told me that she marked "Taxes" or "Household Accounts" on the notebooks she wanted to keep private. Another woman said she hid hers in the laundry room since her husband and children didn't even seem to know the room was there. Whatever works.

I like to write at my computer behind my locked, sound-proof door, but I know people who write in pencil in bus stations or on the back of napkins in restaurants. A poet once told me that she worked between two and four in the morning so she could cry in peace. Some people can only write early in the morning. Find your own best time, your own best way. Adapt the exercises in this book to your own end: do half an exercise, use a technique from one reading and apply it to another, make up your own exercises. The suggestions in this book are meant to inspire you, to get you started, to let you tap into your own creativity. Never let the exercises oppress you. If you ever find yourself saying peevishly, "Well, I don't know what *she* wants me to do in this exercise," put your pen down, close the book.

Think of WORD PLAY/WORD POWER as a user-friendly source book: a book to consult, to enjoy, to "cook" from, to use in any way you wish. Bon appetit.

WRITING ABOUT WRITING

"For me, writing is the only thing that passes the three tests of metier: (1) when I'm doing it, I don't feel that I should be doing something else instead; (2) it produces a sense of accomplishment and, once in a while, pride; and (3) it's frightening."

Gloria Steinam

On the first day in a non-fiction writing class, I usually ask my students to write for 20 minutes on their relationship to writing. The class is required by several different departments in the university, so many of the students are not there by choice. Here are a few of the responses I have received over the past few years.

RELATIONSHIP TO WRITING

When you said get out a piece of paper, my hands started sweating. Then when you said that we were going to write (I'd suspected that you were going to say that) I got butterflies in my stomach. I think I may throw up. I think I may drop this class. I think I may drop out of the university and work in a gas station. It's always been like this when I have to write. Or when I have to write for a teacher. Pure terror takes me over. Pretty soon you'll find out that I can't write. That I can't spell, that I don't know a split infinitive from a banana split. You'll read my papers in front of the class, you'll announce all my errors over the P.A. system during basketball games. There will be noon rallies in front of the student union and I'll be tied up there while you read my horrible, horrible papers. I think I may throw up.

> Education Major (whose flights of imagination
> —and fear—indicate a real writer)

I do not know if I have a relationship with writing. I'm sure I can improve. I am looking forward to this class. Even though I am a business major and this class is required for my major, I am glad that I have to take it. I am sure that you will teach me a lot. I have to make at least a B.

> Business Major (telling me what he thinks
> I want to hear)

I love to write. I would rather write a letter than talk to somebody. I can think about what I want to say in a letter and things go so fast when people talk. My parents are divorced and I write to my father a lot. He doesn't write to me, but he says he likes to get my letters. All the time, I think about what I'll put in the letters. I watch things that happen just so I can tell him about it and sometimes I make it more interesting in the letter that when it really happens. I also love to read.

English Major

I used to like to write. Writing and I had a very positive relationship. Then in the tenth grade, my teacher read one of my papers to the class and trashed it. I thought I was being real philosophical about the existence of God, but she kept talking about overblown ideas and being too abstract. I had been proud of myself for trying to think about these things, I wasn't just showing off. But anyway, that was the end of my good relationship with writing. Every time I try to write now, I feel a little bit afraid. Although as a freshman, I had a good T.A. and she helped me to like writing again. Maybe it is not too late.

Political Science Major

I avoid all classes where I have to do papers. So, I guess my relationship with writing isn't too great. I like to talk, but I don't like to read and don't like to write. I wouldn't be taking this class except that it is either take it or take three quarters of calculus. I don't hate it *that* much.

Business Major

I've always liked to write. My brother taught me how before I started first grade, so I've always felt ahead of other people. I've always made straight A's in English and like to write short stories. It's fun to watch situations and characters sort of grow on paper. It makes me feel like God. I have a whole little kingdom all to myself.

English Major

I always feel I'm doing something wrong when I write. I can't never figure out what, just that the teacher don't like it.

Business Major

I once loved to write. Wrote all of the time, in my journal, for school. I'd write my friends' papers for them, write letters, worked on the city college newspaper, write anything, anywhere. I felt so happy and connected when I wrote. But then I came here and took creative writing. Every paper that I wrote got shot down. The professor wanted everybody to write like Henry James, he read James to us all of the time. I don't like James, really, he's too elaborate. I barely survived that class. Then in the fall, I took another creative writing class and on the first paper, the teacher told me not to imitate James! I'm majoring in science now.

Former English Major

EXERCISE

1. Write for 20 minutes about your relationship to writing.

REAL WRITERS AND TRUST

"Try to be one of the people on whom nothing is lost."
—Henry James, "The Art of Fiction"

I used to think I couldn't be a real writer until I grew up. Then when I grew up, I thought I couldn't really write until I had more experience. More sophistication. More wisdom. Because in order to write, I thought, you had to say something new. How dare I presume at a tender age—at any age, really—to have any worthy secrets?

What I lacked was not experience. It was trust. Trust in my perceptions, in my slim view of the world, in my ability to tell original tales. I didn't, quite simply, trust my *stuff.* I didn't have enough stuff, I supposed; I had to wait until I ripened. When I didn't realize is that if I waited that long I'd fall off the tree and rot.

"Experience," says James, "is never limited, and it is never complete; it is an immense sensibility, a kind of huge spider-web of the finest silken threads suspended in the chamber of consciousness, and catching every airborne particle in its tissue." The curious thing about spider webs in that the light has to be right before one can see them. Writing is such light; it illuminates the web. My fear was that my web wasn't tight or complex enough to have caught more than a few rather large, obvious particles. Who would scramble around my boulders when they could sift through fine, white sand? My web wouldn't bear scrutiny.

Perhaps here is a critical difference between would-be writers and real writers. Real writers either trust that they have something to say, or take a risky leap of faith. They aren't paralyzed, as I was, by audience anxiety. Real writers have a certain shamelessness about their material. "Boulders?" a real writer would ask, "Sure they're boulders, and they're damn good ones!"

But surely some webs catch meatier prey than others. Surely some writers have larger scope, clearer understanding, finer sensibilities! Isn't that why great writers are great? Great writers are great because they write about their subject—whatever it is—with skill and grace. Finesse follows expertise; they write about where they live. A pelican lifts off, flapping awkwardly, from the flat plane of sea, becoming magnificent in flight, winging with the extraordinary elegance a creature can have only at home, in its proper dominion. And so it is with real writers: they take as their subject their own experience. Whether such experience is plucked from one backyard barbecue or gleaned from ten trips around the globe is not important. Pelicans don't consider that eagles soar to loftier heights, and real writers don't get stuck fretting about how others may be smarter, more worldly, more perceptive.

As James says, "impressions *are* experience." We are not limited by the range of our experience, so long as we work up our realm into its fullest conceit. Real writers store impressions, stretching them into harmonious tension; nothing from a life is so base or remote that it cannot somehow be used. Real writers understand the elasticity of experience, and the importance of trust.

Maggie Fox

EXERCISE

1. Write for 20 minutes on writing and trust.

CLUSTERING

Clustering is a widely used technique for getting started in a project. A form of pre-writing, it combines free association and note-taking.

First, jot down your main topic in the center of a sheet of paper. Repeat it over and over to yourself and write in the space around it words or phrases that come to you through free association. Don't edit or think whether or not something is going to fit in later; the object of clustering is simply to get ideas up and out.

For instance, if I were writing a piece on my home town, I would write Santa Barbara in the center of the page and, as I let images and ideas pass through my mind, I'd write down key words to trigger the associations. I might write: beach, State Street, UCSB, thin & blonde, palm trees, beach tar, Tri-County produce, rich, Alice Keck Park, fountains, Mission architecture, have-a-nice-day, gentle, Hwy. 101, 24 Bus, Summer Solstice, Herb & Maggie, Bath Street, Spanish tile, Reagan's ranch, fig tree, Dame Judith Anderson, and so forth. I'd keep on doing this until I began to repeat myself or ran out of space on the paper.

By writing down everything that came into my mind, I have a start for the article. Discarding the useless associations, I could arrange the pertinent ones into an outline if I wished and begin to write. Sometimes in the process of clustering, especially if you are going very quickly, you surprise yourself, make discoveries.

EXERCISES

1. Cluster on your hometown.

2. Cluster on your job.

3. Cluster on yourself.

4. Your essential other.

5. See the BIG PICTURE exercises in Utilizing Your Writing for more on clustering.

FEAR OF WRITING

If you are afraid of writing—and many people are, especially when they first start out—these exercises may help to lessen anxiety. Samples in the first exercise are from students and workshop members.

1. Visualize and describe a private place where you feel safe to write. It may be anywhere—your real writing room, a spot outdoors, somewhere in another dimension. Visualize it in detail. Return to this place each time you begin to write.

EXAMPLES

"My room is big and yellow. I am the only person who is allowed in here. I feel safe here since there are magic bars on the windows to keep out every English teacher I ever had. Nobody can see what I write or how I write in this room."

"My writing room is full of naked women. Tits and ass everywhere. Some of the women are on the waterbed with me and the rest do my writing for me."

"In the entryway into my writing room is a sort of machine that shines light on me as I enter. It isn't exactly light but a technology from another planet that looks like light to us but what is does is to double my intelligence and my concentration. Don't you wish you had one?"

2. Imagine yourself as a kindly, compassionate editor or teacher and give yourself advice on writing.

3. Write as badly as you can. Use every awkward construction, vague reference, and unclear concept you wish. Pile it on. Go on to double negatives, dangling modifiers, split infinitives. Lay into verbs that don't agree, references that don't connect, and the passive voice without end. Write across the margins and upside down on the page. Write until you like the feel of the pen in your hand, until you are having fun. Repeat this exercise every time you sense you are not in control of your writing.

4. Visualize your fear of writing: a teacher with fangs, a professor with a whip, yourself with a copy of Henry James, etc. Give them names and ask them their origins.

5. Talk to these fears. Find out what they want.

6. Visualize a large chest outside of your writing room and, as you enter, put your fears about writing in this chest.

7. Take 20 deep breathes before you start to write.

8. Start with the "Writing for Pleasure" exercises.

9. Visualize a peaceful scene before you begin to write.

10. Set the clock and write non-stop for 20 minutes whether you are afraid or not. If you write through the fear long enough it will go away.

GETTING STARTED ON A POEM

Usually the prime trouble for the unreleased poet (and one lives in all of us) is how to begin, how to take step one in creating a piece of writing that's a poem. As a teacher of writing, I give the following prescription: First, read some poetry—aloud, if possible—by contemporaries, those who will fill your consciousness and heart with the sounds and subjects, the diction, thought, rhythms and reference, of our own wacky times.

Next, take a vow to try not to rhyme. Please? Just for starters? Why? Because if writing poems isn't already as natural for you as a seal sliding into the ocean, playing with rhyme—also with set stanza-structures and metrical notions—may keep you skimming the surface instead of plunging to some personal depth. There will be plenty of time later to toss off some cute limerick or sweat over a sonnet or sestina.

The crucial tool of unstarted *poems* is not a rhyming dictionary. Nor a metronome. Nor rules of any kind. Just the opposite, in fact. If writing-blockage results from fear of failure (as we surely believe it does), from expectation of harsh judgement (usually on the part of the critic who lives in your own ambitious self!), what's needed is relaxation and the willingness to leap off a cliff—verbally speaking, of course.

People of any age who are new to poetry tend to play it safe in a strange way: they'll work at making verses instead of poems, becoming involved with the show-offy sing-song of highly organized language-arrangements (often there's a cute little joke as the so-called subject matter), thereby avoiding the crisis of self-investigation that a poem may bring on by offering neat little da-dum-da-dums instead. It's fun building *verses,* but poems are not essentially verse. Poems are intense and unusual "language acts"—think what a concern for iambic pentameter or "moon/June" can do to subvert that kind of enterprise!

EXERCISE

1. Step one is breathmakingly simple: say a few words, any words. The words "say a few words" will beautifully do. Really, I mean *any* words, absolutely arbitrary words—"absolutely arbitrary" makes a fine example—and set them down AS YOUR FIRST LINE.

Obviously, once you're finished with your draft you're absolutely free to change these first words, remove them altogether maybe, like the scaffolding of a finished building...whatever. It's *your* poem, after all. Sometimes, just for the fun of it, I'll write whatever folks are willing to blurt out in the classroom on the blackboard and say "choose one of these for the first line." Or I'll put down a choice of lines from some striking poems already published (in the long

run you'll drop these borrowings, but they function beautifully for starters).
For example, choose as a first line one of the following:

Hey, not so fast, I don't understand
You mean I should just write anything at all?
I can't think of a word to say, I'm sorry
I was late to class, what's going on?

Or:
Hold, hold it tight
War. She bangs the door
Bedded in the new leaves
They're losing the ways

The first set above, of course, comes from mutterings in a classroom. The second? Arbitrarily, I 've borrowed the third lines of the first four poems in this book.

Now, rapidly, follow up on the chosen first line, let 'er roll, this is only a DRAFT. What do I mean, let 'er roll? Well, if it's really not a line you have the slightest investment in—though something in you picked that one silly way to start over other options, so mysterious depths may already be emerging—why not go on? You can always follow line one with at least one (or two or three or four) more. Watch:

They're losing the ways / like a horse with no rider / running from something / but towards? towards?

They're losing the ways / like a dog with no master....

Continue as long as words appear to extend the first notion with some minimal kind of sense:

With some minimal kind of sense / I slam down any old thing/ look, Ma, no hands! / this here's freewheeling talking....

Please don't worry about the quality of insight, the lilt, the turn of phrase. Later you can brood over word-choice, rhythm, symbol, cutting away the dead parts, making change, choices, rearranging. Now you simply want to keep going. Continuing will lead you somewhere, maybe to those tears, to that surprise. But what if you run out of gas? Most of the time you will go dry, often rather soon. You'll know when it starts to happen: you'll slow down, get bored, blank out, feel strain, disinclination to go any further along this (seemingly) arbitrary line. Aha, now comes tricky step two of the exercise, also intended to relieve you of responsibility for this presumptuous intent to present yourself as a (ahem) poet.

Take one of the first lines you didn't choose—or any line at all—and jot it down at the bottom of the page you've been working on. Here are a set of last line options:

> And that's how it came to an end
> The reasons ran on past knowing
> My mouth fell in love with itself
> I live in that tuna fish can.

Or borrow the fifth, or eighth, line of some of the poems in this book:

> the musicians played instruments of bread
> Kindly remember that.
> understand
> Marble-heavy, a bag full of God

Now, continue developing the thought of the draft you've started so that ending on the chosen line you've written at the bottom of the page will make *some kind of sense.*

See what we're doing? we're combining the arbitrary—even the zany—with some kind of available, reasonable meaningfulness. As Robert Frost puts it: "If it is a wild tune, it is a poem." And: "We enjoy the straight crookedness of a good walking stick." Wild tune. Straight crookedness.

These contradictory supports are what we lean on when we enjoy poetry. Wildness tends toward chaos, the danger of incomprehensibility, untamed eccentricity, astounding but baffling crookedness...hence the need for tune, which is a principle of order, of sanity, of straightness. If it's just a tune, if it's only straight-to-the-point...no tears, laughter, revelation, freshening, surprise. If it's only a wildness, we're lost, pathless. We need both—intent, cause-effect, sequence, "point"—as well as the priceless oddity that marks living language with the unduplicatable flavor of one writer's personality, thought, speech patterns, style, values, concerns.

Give the exercise a chance: let its randomness release tight mental/emotional muscles, and let step two lead you to the excitingly hard work, the exploratory work, of "thinking like a poet" by forging connecting links to bring this little ticking machine of a poem to a halt on just the crazy last line chosen.

Now it's time to look the page over and throw away everything not to your liking. You may be left with only a line, a phrase... or a whole sequence that grabs you. (Once, doing this exercise, I crossed out all but two words before I started again.)

You may want to begin a second draft attempting to weave together the lines you like from draft number one, building a setting for the family jewels the exercise helped you to mine. In some cases you'll discover that you've actually written a finished poem you're proud to recognize as one of your offspring. And if you don't borrow other poet's lines for your first and last, there's no need to find substitutes. In fact, supplying your own firsts and lasts may offer you a method of composition that will keep you writing for a lifetime.

Barry Spacks

WRITING FOR PLEASURE

1. Imagine yourself in a large store—department, sporting goods, antique, restaurant supply, etc. Ten items are free. Describe what you would get.

2. Someone out of your past returns and gives you a gift. Who is it? Describe the gift(s).

3. You can travel to whatever you wish. Go there. Describe what you see and who you meet.

4. You have three wishes. Describe these wishes in detail and their results.

5. You have three wishes to grant to someone else. What are they, for whom, and what are the results?

6. Remember something beautiful. Describe it in detail.

7. You have the power to acquire three new skills. (Playing the violin, becoming psychic, running the mile in less than three minutes, etc.) What are they? What effect do they have on your life?

8. You have the power to instantly speak a foreign language fluently. What is it and what effect does it have on your life?

9. You can change your body in any way you wish. How do you change it? Describe what it feels like to walk around in that body.

10. Overhear a conversation others are having praising you. Report it in detail.

11. You win the lottery: What do you do with the money?

12. List ten books that have influenced you the most. How?

13. Go to any restaurant in the world and order a meal. Do not worry about calories or spelling.

14. Set ten (more or less) realistic goals for yourself. Imagine your life after you have accomplished each of them.

15. You have been given a single dose love potion. What do you do with it?

What are the results?

16. You can eliminate one person on earth without leaving a trace. Who do you pick? Why?

17. You can redo one act from your past. How do you change it? Describe what happens as a result.

18. If you could be another person, who would you be? Why?

19. As that person, perform one act.

20. Describe what you think the world would be like if women were in charge.

21. Create a crowd scene: voices in an airport, restaurant, locker room, etc.

22. Expand your crowd scene and turn it into a short play.

23. Write about the happiest or most satisfying time of your life.

24. Think of someone you love. Write a poem for them.

25. Look at yourself in the mirror. Who or what do you see? Write her or his life story.

26. Look around your living quarters and pick out the objects that have particular meaning for you. Give the history of one of them.

27. If you could go back to one period in history which would you choose? Write a short story set in this time with yourself as the central character.

28. Imagine yourself as the opposite gender. Describe a day in your life.

29. Imagine a bus coming down the road which contains all of your subpersonalities. Watch it come towards you, draw up, then stop. Describe these personalities as they get off the bus. (For example: the efficient businesswoman, the mad poet, the passionate gardener, the angry daughter, the loving friend, etc.)

30. Who from the past would you most like to see again? Describe a meeting with that person.

31. Visualize two people in the distance. Watch as they come towards you. One is you. Who is the other? What are they saying to each other?

32. Conjure up the image of your favorite historical character. Report your conversation with this person.

33. Remember your favorite natural landscape or spot. Describe it as it changes over the seasons.

34. You find a suitcase containing things you have needed or wanted for a long time. Describe each item as you take it out of the suitcase.

35. Make up your own exercise and write for 20 minutes.

WRITING ABOUT WOMEN

"It would be a thousand pities if women wrote like men, or lived like men, or looked like men..."

Virginia Woolf

Writing in his diary before their marriage, Leonard Woolf refers to his future wife, Virginia, as Aspasia. Notice how he begins by describing a landscape, and how he uses nature imagery throughout.

LEONARD ON VIRGINIA

I am in love with Aspasia. . . When I think of Aspasia I think of hills, standing very clear but distant against a cold blue sky; there is snow upon them which no sun has ever melted and no man has ever trodden. But the sun too is in her hair, in the red & the gold of her skin, in the bow of her lips & in the glow of her mind. And most wonderful of all is her voice which seems to bring things from the centre of rocks, deep streams that have lain long in primordial places beneath the earth. To drink once is to be intoxicated for ever. Whether she is walking or sitting there is always about her an air of quiet & clearness, but to think of her is to see her sitting, lying back in immense chairs before innumerable fires. . .

I see her sitting among it all untouched in her quietness & clearness rather silent a little aloof & then the spring bubbles up—is it wit or humour or imagination? I do not know but the thought has come from strange recesses, life for a moment seems to go faster, you feel for a moment the blood in your wrists, your heart beat, you catch your breath as you do on a mountain when suddenly the wind blows. The things that come are strange often fantastic, but they are beautiful & always seem somewhere far below to have touched even to have been torn from reality. Perhaps this is because her mind is so astonishingly fearless, there is no face & no reality which it does not face, touch frankly openly. She is possibly one of three women who know that dung is merely dung, death death & semen semen. She is the most Olympian of the Olympians. And that is why perhaps she seems to take life too hardly. She does not really know the feeling—which alone saves the brain & the body—that after all nothing matters. She asks too much from the earth & the people who crawl about it. I am always frightened that with her eyes fixed on the great rocks she will stumble among the stones.

'And her heart?' you ask. Sometimes I think she has not got one, that she is merely interested in what will happen & in reality, that she is made merely of the eternal snow & the rocks which form the hidden centre of reality. And then I swear that this cannot be true, that the sun in her comes from a heart.

Leonard Woolf
Diary, Quoted in A MARRIAGE OF TRUE MINDS,
by George Spater and Ian Parsons

EXERCISES

1. Describe someone you love. What landscape do they make you think of? Which of their attributes has the strongest effect on you? Like Leonard Woolf in the above passage, try to capture the essence of the person rather than simply giving a physical description.

2. Visualize a loved one. Remember and appreciate his or her special qualities.

Doris Lessing writes here about her cats, but throughout we get a strong sense of her personality as well.

CATS

Grey puss wore her pregnancy lightly. She raced down the garden and up the tree and back; then again, and again; the point of this being the moment when, clamped to the tree, she turned her head, eyes half-closed, to receive applause. She jumped down the stairs three, four at a time. She pulled herself along the floor under the sofa. And, since she had learned that any person, at first sight of her, was likely to go into ecstacies: Oh what a beautiful cat!—she was always near the front door when guests arrived, suitably posed.

Then, trying to slide through banisters to drop onto a stair the flight below, she found she could not. She tried again, could not. She was humiliated, pretended she had not tried, that she preferred walking the long way around the bends in the stairway.

Her rushes up and down the tree became slower, then stopped. And when the kittens moved in her belly, she looked surprised, put out.

Usually, about a fortnight before the birth, a cat will go sniffing into cupboards and corners: trying out, rejecting, choosing. This cat did nothing of the kind. I cleared shoes out of the cupboard in the bedroom, and showed her the place—sheltered, dark, comfortable. She walked into it and out again. Other places were offered. It was not that she did not like them; it seemed that she didn't know what was happening.

The day before the birth, she did roll herself around some old newspapers in a seat, but the actions she used were automatic, nothing purposeful about them. Some gland, or whatever it is, had spoken, prompted movements; she obeyed, but what she did was not connected with her vital knowledge, or so it seemed, for she did not try again.

On the day of the birth she was in labour for three hours or so before she knew it. She miaowed, sounding surprised, sitting on the kitchen floor, and when I ordered her upstairs to the cupboard she went. She did not stay there. She trotted vaguely around the house, sniffing, at this late stage, into various possible places, but lost interest, and came down to the kitchen again. The pain, or sensation, having lessened, she forgot it, and was prepared to start ordinary life again—the life of a pampered, adored kitten. After all, she still was one.

I took her up, and made her stay in the cupboard. She did not want to. She simply did not have any of the expected reactions. In fact, she was touching, absurd—and funny, and we wanted to laugh. When the contractions grew strong, she was cross. When she had a bad pain towards the end, she miaowed, but is was a protesting, annoyed miaow. She was annoyed with us, who concurred in this process being inflicted on her.

It is fascinating to watch the birth of a cat's first kitten, that moment, when, the tiny writhing creature having appeared in its envelope of white cellophane, the cat licks off the covering, nips at the cord, eats the afterbirth, all so cleanly, so efficiently, so perfectly, actions performed by her, personally, for the first time. Always there is a moment of pause. The kitten is expelled, lies at the cat's back end. The cat looks, with a trapped, wanting-to-escape reflex, at the new thing attached to her; she looks again, she does not know what it is; then the mechanism works, and she obeys, becomes mother, purrs, is happy.

With this cat there was the longest pause I've seen while she looked at the new kitten. She looked, looked at me, moved a little, to see if she could lose the attached object—then it worked. She cleaned the kitten, did everything expected of her, purred—and then got up and walked downstairs, where she sat on the back veranda looking at the garden. *That* was over, she seemed to be thinking. Then her sides contracted again, and she turned around to look at me—she was annoyed, furious. Her face, the lines of her body said, unmistakably, What a damned nuisance! Go upstairs! I ordered. Upstairs! She went, sulking. She crept up those stairs with her ears back—almost as a dog does when it is being scolded or in disgrace; but she had none of the abjectness of a dog. On the contrary, she was irritated with me and with the whole process. When she saw the first kitten again, she recognized it, again the machinery worked, and she licked it. She gave birth to four kittens in all, and went to sleep, a charming picture, exquisite cat curled around four feeding kittens. . . .

When the cat woke up, she looked at the kittens, now asleep, got up, shook herself, and strolled downstairs. She drank some milk, ate some raw meat, licked herself all over. She did not go back to the litter.

S. & H., coming to admire the kittens found mamma cat, posed on the bottom of the stairs in profile. Then she ran out of the house, up the tree and back again—several times. Then she went up to the top of the house, and came all the way down by dropping through the banisters of one flight, to the flight below. Then she wove around H.'s legs, purring.

"You are supposed to be a mother," said S., shocked. "Why aren't you with your kittens?"

It seemed she had forgotten the kittens. Inexplicably, she had had an uncomfortable job to do; she had done it; it was over, and that was that. She frisked and frolicked around the house until, late that night, I ordered her upstairs. She would not go. I picked her up and carried her to the kittens. With no grace at all, she got in with them. She would not lie down to feed them. I made her. As soon as I turned away, she left them. I sat with her as she fed them.

I went to get ready for bed. When I came back to the bedroom, she was under my sheet, asleep. I returned her to the kittens. She looked at them with her ears back, and again would have simply walked off, if I had not stood over her, pointing, inexorable figure of authority, at the kittens. She went in, slumped down, as if to say, if you insist. Once the kittens were at her nipples instinct did work, even if ineffectually, and she purred for a while.

All through the night she was sneaking out of the cupboard and getting into her usual place on my bed. Every time I made her go back. As soon as I was asleep, back she came, while the kittens complained.

She had understood, by morning, that she was responsible for those kittens. But left to herself, that great Mother, nature, notwithstanding, she would let them starve.

Doris Lessing
PARTICULARLY CATS

EXERCISES

1. Write a short biography of your cat, dog, or other pet. Remember that every biography includes at least two people: the person being written about and the writer. Try, as Lessing does, to observe closely your pet's actions or reactions to a particular event.

2. Write about yourself from your pet's point of view. As you do so, try to become your pet; find a voice that embodies its personality; imagine into what name or names your pet might call you.

3. Answer the question: Do you think there is such a thing as maternal instinct.

*Our own culture has no poetic image, no song for a girl's first men-
struation, no way of marking this event. The following song from
New Guinea depicts a stark, even violent, change as the white
eel—girlhood—is replaced by the black crayfish of womanhood.*

SONG FOR A GIRL
ON HER FIRST MENSTRUATION

Hold, hold it tight,
grasp the black crayfish,
hold, hold it tight.
Grab the white eel.
Sisirik, Miampa lumbo
Grasp the black crayfish
Kayame Parilumpo
kill the white eel.

> Anonymous, New Guinea, Joe Prentuo, Translator
> THE OTHER VOICE: 20th Century Women's Poetry
> in Translation ed. Joanna Bankier, et al

EXERCISES

1. Write about your first menstruation. You might want to write symbolically
as in the New Guinea song or tell about the actual event. Many of us have stories
that involve embarrassment, confusion, shame, and—especially in
retrospect—humor.

2. Write about how you would (or have) explained menstruation to your girl
child. Now write how you would tell a boy.

Matrophobia is not the fear of one's mother as you first might think, but the fear of becoming one's mother.

MATROPHOBIA

Until I entered therapy, I thought I hated my mother because she set herself up to be first a victim, then a martyr. Later I realized it wasn't my mother I hated, but my own capacity to become her. I saw how much of my life had gone into acting as differently from her as possible. Unconsciously I'd keep my apartment messy, be terribly disorganized, or run late in contra-distinction to her excessive neatness, order, and tendency to arrive early. But I wasn't free of her, wasn't actualizing myself, but simply becoming her opposite, her mirror image.

It took me a long time to face the fact that I used anger (usually righteous) to shield my real feelings, and that my beloved hatred masked the terror of giving into my pull towards her. In my panic, I felt I had to reject her completely in order to purge from my very bones what she had transmitted to me about being a woman.

Ellen Amber
HOW I GOT FROM THERE TO HERE

EXERCISES

1. Describe a matrophobic response: yours, a friend's, your daughter's.

2. Make a list of all the ways you and your mother are similar.

3. Make another list of how you are different.

Many people keep a travel journal when they take a trip. Fewer people have thought to do the same as they journey through the strange and wondrous landscape of pregnancy and childbirth.

MOTHERHOOD

January 6, 1978

Midnight. It's not working. *I'm* not working. I have no "overwhelming urge" to push. I want to give up, to give you up; to give birth. But I can't.

"Take the breath and hold it when the contraction starts," Shifra says. "Otherwise it's not effective."

Just give me a minute to rest. But you don't. You keep coming. There are so many pinpoints, all light-years away; galactic opening for you to enter through. I keep missing you. . . What if I catch someone else?

Your longest journey is so short. How many inches must you actually cross over into being? Don't be frightened. Someday this journey will end. This journey never ends. I'm filled with pity and terror for you.

Which one of us is being born? . . .

January 12, 1978

You fall on my breast, fiercely, like a lion. When you lose my nipple, you rage, grow desperate. Sightless, you burrow for it in my shoulder, under my breast. Frantic, ridiculous.

This is a matter of life and death for you. You clarify human nature for me.

Such peace, when I breast-feed you. Such pleasure! When you put a hand to my nipple, I tingle, I flush. There is no end, no rude climax to this sensation. You suck on my nipple and I feel it in my clitoris and all along my soul.

When will you and I be satisfied like this again?

July 20, 1978

Suddenly I find myself thinking about my mother. How is she? What is she doing? I pick up the phone and find out. *I feel close to her for the first time in my life.*

I can't be like my mother. I can't allow myself to be swallowed up by either the experience or the institution of motherhood. My mother's behavior shows me, too clearly, the horrible price it exacted of her.

I feel close to my mother. . . .No. Becoming a mother somehow allows me to admit, to act on, what I've always felt: my love for her.

This is incredible! *I love my mother.* I've never said this to her. She's never said it to me. We're not friends. . . .

> Phyllis Chesler
> WITH CHILD
> A DIARY OF MOTHERHOOD

EXERCISE

1. Write your own diary of motherhood, of your experiences during pregnancy, childbirth, and mothering. Include and leave out whatever you wish. You might consider telling at least a part of the story from your child's point of view. If you've never had a child, imagine the situation and describe the experience.

2. Tell the story of your own birth as told to you by your mother.

Note how the simple, direct language in the following poem carries the feeling of distilled, primitive, emotion. The intensely expressed hatred in the poem also reveals an involvement so total it could just as well be love.

MOTHERS, DAUGHTERS

Through every night we hate,
preparing the next day's
war. She bangs the door.
Her face laps up my own
despair, the sour, brown eyes,
the heavy hair she won't
tie back. She's cruel,
as if my private meanness
found a way to punish us.
We gnaw at each other's
skulls. Give me what's mine.
I'd haul her back, choking
myself in her, herself
in me. There is a book
called *Poisons* on her shelf.
Her room stinks with incense,
animal turds, hamsters
she strokes like silk. They
exercise on the bathroom
floor, and two drop through
the furnace vent. The whole
house smells of the accident,
the hot skins, the small
flesh rotting. Six days
we turn the gas up then
to fry the dead. I'd fry
her head if I could until
she cried love, love me!

All she won't let me do.
Her stringy figure in
the windowed room shares
its thin bones with no one.

Only her shadow on the glass
waits like an older sister.
Now she stalks, leans forward,
concentrates merely on getting
from here to there. Her feet
are bare. I hear her breathe
where I can't get in. If I
break through to her, she will
drive nails into my tongue.

Shirley Kaufman
THE FLOOR KEEPS TURNING

EXERCISES

1. Write a poem about your mother. Try to get at the underlying emotion(s) you
feel towards her. It doesn't have to be negative, of course, nor even intense. But
try to let the language you use convey the emotion you feel.

2. Visualize your mother. Try to feel her presence and enter into a dialogue with
her. What did you say?

MOTHER-DAUGHTER FIGHTS

1956. A suburb in Queens, as far from Manhattan as Peoria, Illinois, was. In the kitchen, where so many mother-daughter dramas unroll. Everywhere, in the lighted windows of two-story, red brick houses, women stand over their sinks, finishing washing the dishes of the evening meal. The fathers have sunk into armchairs in front of the television sets. The brothers are out toting the garbage or dashing to basketball practice. I, a daughter of sixteen, and my mother of forty-three are having a discussion that begins quietly, full of tension. The situation is simple: I have been invited by my boyfriend to Fall Weekend at Cornell. This means a great deal in the world of adolescence. As I must, I am asking my mother's permission and my mother is refusing.

Foot-binder.

Mothers are the ones who stamp out the flowers.

Corset. Straitjacket.

"Let me out to the night." As Anna Wickham cried in a poem, "Let me go, let me go."

The mother has been charged with control of these things. She wants her daughter to "behave" because a badly behaved daughter means, in the mother's world, a failed mother. Sex is in mind. She imagines beer brawls and orgies—this is what is in the popular mind about such events as fall weekends at Cornell. (She knows the boy; she likes the boy; she cannot match the boy with orgies, but she sets that aside.) Sex troubles her in her own life; it troubles her in relation to her daughter in ways she cannot begin to think of.

Mother as Tree of Life.

Mother the protector, caretaker, nurturer.

To keep the child from harm. To protect her, even at the risk of her own life. To sense danger, as an animal does, and shield the young.

The mother says you cannot go and the daughter says why not and the mother falls back to parent language to say because I said so and the daughter presses and the mother says because and the daughter, more agitated, more provocative, insists WHY and the mother says that thing about "nice girls don't" and the daughter wants to be nice because her mother will love her if she is nice but wants to see Cornell and be with Robert and tell her friends she has been at a college weekend. . .

All the time, the mother is bending over the kitchen sink, washing the dishes. On the wall above her is a magnetic knife rack and five gleaming blades.

There is blood swirling between them. The daughter goes blind and out of her senses. Her hand is tight around the handle of the knife and her arm is raised—all very quickly—over her mother's bent head and shoulders. She grazes the bone at the top of her mother's spine.

Louise Bernikow
AMONG WOMEN

EXERCISES

1. Describe a fight with your mother.

2. Tell the fight from her point of view.

The word "love" is never mentioned in this passage, but it seems to shimmer around every word, to create a kind and trusting atmosphere in which the mother and children interact.

MOTHER LOVE

At night with the lights out, after she had heard our prayers, my mother would sing to James and me, and we thought she was great. She'd sing "Down by the Old Mill Stream" or some Cole Porter she knew from college. She loved Frank Sinatra. She would stand by our bed, crooning imitations into one of the bedposts as if it were a microphone, and afterward we would clap in the dark until our hands stung. (At the end of "Pennies from Heaven," she would place a penny on each post for us to find in the morning.) "Thank you, thank you," she would whisper with a low, wonderful laugh, smiling and bending over us to wetly kiss our cheeks, her hair down, long, black, and sweeping against my chest and chin, smelling soapy and dry. And if the moon was out it lit up the lake, and the light shone into the room through the slats of the blinds, tentatively striping her hair and face or the arm of her sweater. And as she moved—to kiss James, to tuck in the blankets—the stripes moved up and down her. When she left she always kept the door slightly unlatched, the lamp from the hall framing the door in cracks of light interrupted only by hinges. She always called in a whisper, "Good night my sweet sparrows," that expression only later in my life seeming silly or indulgent or mad. And often James would be on his back next to me humming late into the night, invisible in the dark, singing the words to "Old Devil Moon" when he could remember them, or sometimes just whispering, "Hey, Lynnie, how does it go again?" his legs jiggling under the sheets.

Lorrie Moore
SELF-HELP

EXERCISES

1. Remember a scene in which you felt most connected with your mother—bedtime, mealtime, whatever. Recreate it as lovingly as possible.

2. Visualize your mother laughing. Recall a time when the two of you had a good laugh over something together.

*Note how important the season of fall becomes in this poem, and
how describing the season leads the poem's voice toward personal
concerns.*

REAP AND CARRY

The first day of fall
and my delphiniums are firmly
bedded in, the new leaves
already bold.

Evening comes earlier
as I walk from work in the cool,
lengthening shadows, past gardens
I've memorized, and my half-way mark:
a leaf fossil in cement.

This season brings childhood back
with its quickening, sharp air:
I felt it biking home after raking leaves,
earned coins clicking in my pockets
with a sound of small bells.

Season of school: I drew maps and gave
each bird, each crop, its rightful place.
I can still chant *Kansas wheat,
Georgia peaches, Idaho potatoes.*

Fall, and I am a woman who gardens
for hours forgetting meal
In this faithful time of planting
we make love for a child.

I lay papery bulbs in the narrow cups
my hands have dug.
I am deliberate and expectant
and wait for the jonquil's
hardy, brimming spine.

Lauren Mesa
SPECTRUM

EXERCISES

1. Write about wanting a baby.

2. Write about your garden. Describe your favorite gardening activity—planting,
weeding, watering, whatever—and how it makes you feel.

Motherhood is a subject which is difficult to demystify, hard to write about without falling into cliche, simplification, or generalization. Here Susan Griffin explores the complexity and contradictions of the subject.

FEMINISM AND MOTHERHOOD

On this subject—Feminism and Motherhood—very little has been written.

I am hesitant to begin anywhere. My words come up out of frustration. They are often blurted out. And then I do not record them. What is said must be so right. Guilt surrounds me. I am angry at my mother for not mothering me. There, it is said. I am angry—this is harder to say—at my daughter for always interrupting me. Generation after generation it is the same story. My daughter says to me one night, 'You don't like me because I always bother you.' I carry this around with me, these words, a sorrow so deep to express it would be to fly apart.

I have been asked if I had the choice again, would I have a child? This is an absurd question. I am not the same person I was before I had a child. That young woman would not understand me.

What did you learn from having a child?
    I learned vulnerability. So simple, really, the simplicity of it amazed me, tears, my daughter's tears, her pain, her fears, and that I could comfort her, that her body relaxed against mine, that she learned to smile from me, that she was wholly unashamed of her hungers, her tempers, that there was no line of explanation between joy and sorrow but experience itself. The vulnerability and the clear logic of her flesh was a revelation to me. One morning, shortly after her birth, I lay on top of the bed crying because I realized one day I would have to explain death to her. Clearly in all her innocence, she did not deserve death. . . .

Is it because no one shares the daily work of raising a child with me? I ask. Or have I changed? Is it because I have too much work and too little time? Or because I myself feel unloved. Or tired. Now I am quarrelling with myself and I am not accusing myself of spoiling her. I don't listen enough, I tell myself. I don't spend enough time with her; I have this argument with myself as I try to make telephone calls, do laundry, write out the bills, grade papers, type poems or letters, and she is running in and out of the room with questions and demands. I call them interruptions.

Very little has been written on the subject of motherhood.

What did you learn from having a child?
    I was all alone all day in the house with an infant. I began to watch daytime television. I watched soap operas. Women are always having surgery on daytime TV. I began to identify with those women. I began to feel as if I had had a lobotomy. I had always relied on being able to sleep long hours before. Now my daughter woke me every three hours. I had loved conversation before. Now I was alone in a house with an infant most of the time. And when I went out, always with my child and husband (I did not exist apart from them), I found I had lost my speech. I was inarticulate. I imagined people thought me stupid. I felt stunned, dumb. But there was something I had wanted to tell. Something profound.

    I learned what it is like not to be able to speak.

Birthing, raising my daughter through infancy to childhood was a hard process of knowledge, a kind of physical endurance for us both, bearing knowledge of survival; of the simplest facts of eating, sleeping, and the struggle to exist. All around me floated archetypal mothers, Italian Madonnas, the red velvet framing their breasts as unstained as their smiles, young, carefree-looking women running in slow motion across fields, swooping to caress angelic children, unbearably lithe models grinning over clean babies in clean blankets. I could not see through them. My own experience waited blind and dumb, unspoken.

I don't have a feminist theory of motherhood. I have only these notes, these paragraphs, some insights. Curiously, they take the form of another woman's writing about motherhood, *Momma,* by Alta: she has two young children. They take the form of Rene Clair's 'Leaves of Hypnos',the journal he wrote during the French Resistance. We are part of a resistance. For necessity does not stop long enough for us to analyze. We have only brief illuminations which we must record between interruptions, set down side by side, hoping to make sense of it all some day later.

    And scrutiny is painful. Society's suggestion of guilt is involved. And too much suffocation. Too many contradictions. So that when a woman is finally free of her children's needs, she wants to forget. She does not want to face or express her rage. And rage must come before analysis. Even now I feel I want to escape this. It is said, 'I do not want to think about my children now.'

Susan Griffin
MADE FROM THIS EARTH

EXERCISES

1. What did you learn from having a child? You might want to ask the question over and over as Susan Griffin does, giving a series of answers—all of which are true, but none of which are complete.

2. Visualize yourself as the mother of a baby, a child, a teenager, an adult with children.

SINGLE PARENTING

1976:

Woke up alone in bed: teenagers with pubescent sidekicks taken over house. Walk from room to room: noise, rock albums everywhere. Old Kentucky Fried Chicken boxes spread greasy spots on the sofa. Three-year-old sword mark on grey plaster wall where daughter's boyfriend, drunk, dancing on top of the Chinese teak bar, slashed it with Grandfather's saber. Whines and snivels and moans. They want money, more *things*.

They're not *my* kids," he said, just before he left.

I would never have dared have that kind of party in my mother's house. But my mother ran the family outpost like a military camp. Nothing ever out of place. Wasn't that what I was trying to get away from when I began my great liberation? Away from middle class order? From repressive, domesticated sexuality? So what happened? How did I end up living here in a cross between K-Mart and Beirut?

Oh. Right. Sex.

Sex that led to children. That's the part we forgot back in the sixties when we were young and beautiful and believed we'd be that way forever: who'd raise the children. But we hadn't had them yet. Or maybe we assumed human babies were more malleable than they turned out to be.

Single parenthood sucks. Can only be half a mother, half a father. Half crazy.

Sit down. Think.

Don't blame feminism. Take responsibility. I can't wait for the feminist revolution to come and solve my problems. We *are* the revolution. Yes I know. The personal *is* political.

Right.

But burnout strips away all ideology; exhaustion rages. Why is every day life so hard? Money, child care, structures all set up for patriarchal relationships, not for single mothers. Theory doesn't help. Fuck theory. Theory got me where I am: desperate, cut off, suicidal.

With no one to blame but myself.

Personal life gone long ago. Nothing left to give up. Still not enough time, not enough energy.

1986:

My daughter cries to her therapist that I wasn't there for her. (As if I had been there for myself.) But she says I didn't provide this, didn't do that. My daughter, the victim.

Tried to break the pattern, to create a new type of life, one without so much guilt and manipulation between mother and daughter. Thinking if I just did the opposite of what my mother did to me, then we'd be fine, my daughters and I. It worked with one. Backfired with the other.

Wake up to find myself manipulated by my daughter, stolen from her, abused, rejected.

Just as I abused and rejected my own mother. Just as my daughter says I abused and rejected her.

Mirror, mirror on the wall.

There's more.
Living out changes
in our bodies, in our minds, in our daughters' lives.
Karma.
Be careful. Think.

Joan Snider
COLD AND HOWLING HELLS

EXERCISES

1. Make a list of all the things that are against you (or your mother) as a single parent.

2. Make another list of the advantages of being a single parent.

3. Write the history of yourself as a mother; then, as a father. Compare the two roles.

Notice the wonderful use of concrete detail in this passage and the way in which the mother is brought alive, especially as she tells her monkey story.

MOTHER'S COOKING

My mother has cooked for us: raccoons, skunks, hawks, city pigeons, wild ducks, wild geese, blackskinned bantams, snakes, garden snails, turtles that crawled about the pantry floor and sometimes escaped under refrigerator or stove, catfish that swam in the bathtub. "The emperor used to eat the peaked hump of purple dromedaries," she would say. "They used chopsticks made from rhinoceros horn, and they ate ducks' tongues and monkeys' lips." She boiled the weeds we pulled up in the yard. There was a tender plant with flowers like white stars hiding under the leaves, which were like the flower petals but green. I've not been able to find it since growing up. It had no taste. When I was as tall as the washing machine, I stepped out on the back porch one night, and some heavy, ruffling, windy, clawed thing dived at me. Even after getting chanted back to sensibility, I shook when I recalled that perched everywhere there were owls with great hunched shoulders and yellow scowls. They were a surprise for my mother from my father. We children used to hide under the beds with our fingers in our ears to shut out the bird screams and the thud, thud of the turtles swimming in the boiling water, their shells hitting the sides of the pot. Once the third aunt who worked at the laundry ran out and bought us bags of candy to hold over our noses; my mother was dismembering skunk on the chopping block. I would smell the rubbery odor through the candy.

In a glass jar on a shelf my mother kept a big brown hand with pointed claws stewing in alcohol and herbs. She must have brought it from China because I do not remember a time when I did not have the hand to look at. She said it was a bear's claw, and for many years I thought bears were hairless. My mother used the tobacco, leeks, and grasses swimming about the hand to rub our sprains and bruises.

Just as I would climb up to the shelf to take one look after another at the hand, I would hear my mother's monkey story. I'd take my fingers out of my ears and let her monkey words enter my brain. I did not always listen voluntarily, though. She would begin telling the story, perhaps repeating it to a homesick villager, and I'd overhear before I had a chance to protect myself. Then the monkey words would unsettle me; a curtain flapped loose inside my brain. I have wanted to say, "Stop it. Stop it," but not once did I say, "Stop it."

"Do you know what people in China eat when they have the money?" my mother began. "They buy into a monkey feast. The eaters sit around a thick wood table with a hole in the middle. Boys bring in the monkey at the end of a pole. Its neck is in a collar at the end of the pole, and it is screaming. Its hands are tied behind it. They clamp the monkey into the table; the whole table fits like another collar around its neck. Using a surgeon's saw, the cooks cut a clean line in a circle at the top of its head. To loosen the bone, they tap with a tiny hammer and wedge here and there with a silver pick. Then an old woman reaches out her hand to the monkey's face and up to its scalp, where she tufts some hairs and lifts off the lid of the skull. The eaters spoon out the brains."

Did she say, "You should have seen the faces the monkey made"? Did she say, "The people laughed at the monkey screaming"? It was alive? The curtain flaps closed like merciful black wings.

"Eat! Eat!" my mother would shout at our heads bent over bowls, the blood pudding awobble in the middle of the table.

She had one rule to keep us safe from toadstools and such: "If it tastes good, it's bad for you," she said. "If it tastes bad, it's good for you."

We'd have to face four- and five-day old leftovers until we ate it all. The squid eye would keep appearing at breakfast and dinner until eaten. Sometimes brown masses sat on every dish. I have seen revulsion on the faces of visitors who've caught us at meals.

"Have you eaten yet?" the Chinese greet one another.

"Yes, I have," they answer whether they have or not. "And you?"

I would live on plastic.

Maxine Hong Kingston
THE WOMAN WARRIOR

EXERCISES

1. Describe your mother's cooking, her attitude towards food, and its effect on you. Be specific and concrete. Perhaps you might want to concentrate on one particular meal, an imaginary event made up of all the real meals, cooked and served by your mother. By combining a variety of different elements from many occasions into a fictionalized meal, you are more likely to get at the essence of the subject than if you plod through being true to each historic fact.

2. Visualize your mother in the kitchen as she cooks and serves food. Compare this to the way you function in the kitchen.

BREAD

It was the anniversary of bread
the bread-celebration
on that day everything was bread
mattresses pillows blankets chairs
windows
(wanting to look out, the child
chewed a hole in the bread pane)
the musicians played instruments of bread
the mayor unveiled
a bread monument
in honor of bread

People came from every corner of the republic
laughing and pushing, crowding in the streets
a busload of pickpockets emptied itself in the square
everyone wanted the bread
that thrust up on long stalks from the ground, or
hung down on strings from the sky

This bread was of three kinds
yellow, with raisins
like little black buttons
or pink as the sunset
or white as a girl's veil
at her first communion
—it made no difference
the people ate it all

Riding out into the dusk
the buses were filled with bread
the roads were lined with bread
the people waved
Goodbye, goodbye to the bread
they were chewing and laughing
in the deserted streets maybe one or two
were left lying asprawl
pillowed in a doorway, dead-drunk on bread
under stars clustered thick as raisins

Constance Urdang
A GEOGRAPHY OF POETS

EXERCISES

1. Celebrate a food in a poem. Experiment with Constance Urdang's technique of using repetition and wild flights of the imagination to create a comic effect.

2. Write about making bread. Write about what the dough feels like in your hands, how it smells when it's baking, the effect it has on others when you give it to them warm from the oven.

The absence of any capital letters or punctuation in this poem intensifies the sense that the people involved are outsiders.

the way & the way things are

gramma thinks about her grandchildren
they're losing the ways
don't know how to talk indian
don't understand me when
i ask for tobacco
don't know how to skin a rabbit
sad sad
they're losing the ways

but gramma
you told your daughters
marry white men
told them they would have
nicer houses
fancy cars
pretty clothes
could live in the city

gramma your daughters did
they couldn't speak indian anymore
how could we grandchildren learn
there are no rabbits to skin
in the city
we have no gramma there to
teach us the ways

you were still on the reservation
asking somebody anybody
please
get me tobacco

Nila northSun
DIET PEPSI AND NACHO CHEESE

EXERCISES

1. Write about the way things are with your grandmother. Since most people have two grandmothers, you might want to compare their situations, their attitudes, their effect on you.

2. From your grandmother's point of view, write about losing the old ways.

The following are excerpts from student papers.

ABORTION

When the home pregnancy test came out positive, I did nothing but cry for a week, then went through all this stuff, saying that I couldn't do it, that I'd have the baby. I went around to all the stores and looked at the little pink booties, and got all sentimental about everything. My boyfriend didn't seem very enthusiastic about a baby, but said that he would "do the right thing." So then I got on my high horse and said that he didn't have to marry me, that I'd have the baby on my own, raise it by myself. Then I finally realized what it would do to my life, how disappointed my family would be if I quit college, how I didn't really want to be a single mom. The abortion itself was a real relief, and I've never regretted making that decision.

***

I got pregnant when I was almost 40, after I'd already raised two children and gotten them into high school. During my freshman year in college, I'd gotten pregnant and had to get married and drop out of school. Ironically, I'd just started back to college when I got pregnant last year. No way was I going to start all over with another baby. I'm only glad that abortions were legal when I needed one this time.

***

My boyfriend wasn't at all supportive when I told him that I was going to have a baby. He didn't even want to pay anything towards the abortion, even though he was the one who didn't like to use condoms. In the end, I had to get a girlfriend to drive me to the clinic. We broke up right after that.

***

I couldn't believe it when I got pregnant and had to have an abortion. I just didn't think that my body would do that to me. I'm still mad about it.

***

After my abortion, I didn't feel bad for myself or for the foetus, I just didn't want my ultra-religious family to find out about it. They wouldn't understand at all. Every time I hear my Mom talk about how they should make abortions illegal, I cringe inside, but I'll never, ever tell her that I had one.

***

The abortion hurt a lot more than I thought it would. They said that I wouldn't be able to feel it, but I did. I sure as hell did. The people at the clinic—especially this one nurse—were real mean to me. She kept saying that I shouldn't be able to feel anything, but I knew what I felt. The whole experience was one that I don't intend to repeat.

***

When my girlfriend told me that she was pregnant, I got real excited. I thought it would be great to get married and have a kid, but she didn't. She made an appointment for the abortion right away—we hardly talked about it. I supported her decision and all, but I felt very disappointed.

***

I've had three abortions. I knew I didn't want children (I sort of wanted the first, but he didn't, so it wasn't a real possibility to have a child at that time). Anyway, abortions seemed to be these necessary things that I went through. I didn't think much about them at the time or afterwards, and didn't think that they affected me very much. But one day, out of the blue, all the stuff that I'd pushed down about the abortions just came whooshing up into consciousness, and I sobbed out loud for almost two hours straight. Until that time, I would have sworn that having those abortions hadn't really bothered me at all.

EXERCISES

1. Describe your abortion, how you felt when you found out you were pregnant, the process you went through, the abortion itself and the aftermath.

2. Imagine yourself pregnant and considering an abortion.

3. From the prospective father's point of view, write an account of a woman who decides to have (or not have) an abortion.

This poem achieves an ironic effect by coupling a voice which "officially" forgives with a voice which retracts.

I FORGIVE YOU

I forgive you, Maria,
Things can never be the same,
But I forgive you, Maria,
Though I think you were to blame.
I forgive you, Maria,
I never can forget,
But I forgive you, Maria,
Kindly remember that.

Stevie Smith
ME AGAIN

EXERCISES

1. Write about someone you have forgiven or someone who has forgiven you. Experiment with the use of two voices.

2. Make a list of people you've never forgiven and their offenses.

LOVE EVERLASTING

Research shows that there are couples who seem to bond immediately: they often report that they "recognize" each other within 15 minutes, and decide to spend the rest of their lives together. After that, they are only apart for a day or two when she's in the hospital having children. For the next 60 years, they behave like lovers. They'll sit side by side on the sofa rather than in separate chairs—so they can hold hands. Also there's an enormous degree of communication and sensitivity between them. Each knows without being told how the other feels. Throughout their life together, they feel uncomfortable when they are apart and happy when together.

Although scientists can document what prevents us from forming this kind of bond—fear of intimacy, ambivalence, lack of trust—they don't know exactly what allows the attachment to take place in certain couples. Often a romantic relationship ends when reality triumphs over fantasy, but with these bonded pairs, it is as if the reality is better than the fantasy. Rather than being disappointed in the other person, they claim to be constantly surprised at how wonderful their partner is.

They very rarely quarrel, and tend to make up quickly. Distance is very painful to them, so they are highly motivated to prevent or patch up a fight. It's not that they are unaware of each other's faults, but they don't emphasize them. There's total acceptance of each other. Total.

Furthermore, research shows that they are very sexual with each other as well as strongly monogamous. They simply aren't interested in other people. Perhaps there might be one or two extramarital affairs over the period of a lifetime, but they tend to report these as negative experiences. Willing monogamy is much more the rule: like geese or wolves who mate for a lifetime. (Other couples seem "naturally" promiscuous like rabbits or chimpanzees where the male chases anything in heat.)

The bond between these couples seems as strong as—and very similar to—the bond between mother and child. Similar in the sense of an unspoken, emotional connection between the two that is profound.

H.D. Starr

EXERCISES

1. Describe your relationship with your significant other in the light of this essay. How similar are you to the closely bonded couple described here? How far away?

2. Would you like to be that closely bonded? Why or why not?

As in many of Dorothy Parker's poems, the twist at the end turns a seemingly sentimental approach on its head.

PICTURES IN THE SMOKE

Oh, gallant was the first love, and glittering and fine;
The second love was water, in a clear white cup;
The third love was his, and the fourth mine;
And after that, I always get them all mixed up.

Dorothy Parker
THE COLLECTED POETRY
OF DOROTHY PARKER

EXERCISES

1. Describe your first love in detail.

2. Make a list of your loves in chronological order. Be careful where you leave the list.

3. Write a short poem to your favorite love.

A teacher receives many interesting notes from students during her career. The following is one of my own favorites.

RELATIONSHIPS

"My relationship prevented me from coming to class today."
Student, University of California at Santa Barbara

EXERCISES

1. Define relationship.

2. List and describe five major relationships you've had in your life. Look for patterns.

3. Imagine life without relationships. Describe a day in that life.

4. Which of your relationships has been the most satisfying? Why?

5. Which of your relationships has been the most destructive? Why?

6. Make a time chart of your relationships. Do not cheat.

7. Pick one relationship and describe your part in it from the other person's point of view.

8. What do you expect from a relationship?

9. What do you contribute to a relationship?

10. How do relationships end with you? How would you like for them to end?

LITANY OF THE GOOD WIFE

I must pretend to be happy when I am not; for everyone's sake.

I must make no adverse comment on the manner of my existence; for everyone's sake.

I must be grateful for the roof over my head and the food on my table, and spend my days showing it, by cleaning and cooking and jumping up and down from my chair; for everyone's sake.

I must make my husband's parents like me, and my parents like him; for everyone's sake.

I must consent to the principle that those who earn most outside the home deserve most inside the home; for everyone's sake.

I must build up my husband's sexual confidence, I must not express any sexual interest in other men, in private or in public. I must ignore his way of diminishing me by publicly praising women younger, prettier, and more successful than I, and sleeping with them in private, if he can; for everyone's sake.

I must render him moral support in all his undertakings, however immoral they may be, for the marriage's sake. I must pretend in all matters to be less than he; for everyone's sake.

I must love him through wealth and poverty, through good times and bad, and not swerve in my loyalty to him, for everyone's sake.

Fay Weldon
THE LIFE AND LOVES OF A SHE-DEVIL

EXERCISES

1. Describe your feelings as you read the above litany.

2. Create your own Litany of a Good_____ . Fill in the blank with an appropriate word and write with an appropriate edge.

The anarchist Emma Goldman had a series of very intense relationships with a number of men during her lifetime. "I can't help it," she complained, "if men can't keep up with me."

MARRIAGE AND LOVE

The popular notion about marriage and love is that they are synonymous, that they spring from the same motives, and cover the same human needs. Like most popular notions this also rests not on actual facts, but on superstition.

Marriage and love have nothing in common; they are as far apart as the poles; are, in fact, antagonistic to each other. No doubt some marriages have been the result of love. Not, however, because love could assert itself only in marriage; much rather is it because few people can completely outgrow a convention. There are today large numbers of men and women to whom marriage is naught but a farce, but who submit to it for the sake of public opinion. At any rate, while it is true that some marriages are based on love, and while it is equally true that in some cases love continues in married life, I maintain that it does so regardless of marriage, and not because of it.

On the other hand, it is utterly false that love results from marriage. On rare occasions one does hear of a miraculous case of a married couple falling in love after marriage, but on close examination, it will be found that it is a mere adjustment to the inevitable. Certainly the growing-used to each other is far from the spontaneity, the intensity, and beauty of love, without which the intimacy of marriage must prove degrading to both the woman and the man.

Marriage is primarily an economic arrangement, an insurance pact. It differs from the ordinary life insurance agreement only in that it is more binding, more exacting. Its returns are insignificantly small compared with the investments. In taking out an insurance policy one pays for it in dollars and cents, always at liberty to discontinue payments. If, however, woman's premium is a husband, she pays for it with her name, her privacy, her self-respect, her very life, "until death doth part." Moreover, the marriage insurance condemns her to life-long dependency, to parasitism, to complete uselessness, individual as well as social. Man, too, pays his toll, but as his sphere is wider, marriage does not limit him as much as woman. He feels his chains more in an economic sense.

Thus Dante's motto over Inferno applies with equal force to marriage: "Ye who enter here leave all hope behind."

> Emma Goldman (1917), THE TRAFFIC IN WOMEN
> AND OTHER ESSAYS ON FEMINISM

EXERCISES

1. Comment on your own marriage (or your parents') in light of Emma Goldman's essay.

2. Write about the essay itself—its attitude towards marriage, towards women. What do you think of Emma Goldman's opinions?

In this novel, in accordance with a decree of "the Providers," Al•Ith, ruler of Zone Three, a pastoral, feminist land, has recently married Ben Ata, ruler of the war-oriented Zone Four.

MARRIAGE

As Al•Ith swung there, lightly, and delightfully, on her pillar, smiling, and waiting, he understood that he was now to start again. There was no help for it. He could not refuse, for his month as apprentice, and a willing one, had already said yes to what was to come.

As he challenged and antagonized, an equal—at the same time his look at Al•Ith told her all this. And so she left her pillar, and came to him, and began to teach him how to be equal and ready in love.

It was quite shocking for him, because it laid him open to pleasures he had certainly not imagined with Elys [a Zone Four courtesan]. There was no possible comparison between the heavy sensualities of that, and the changes and answering of these rhythms. He was laid open not only to physical responses he had not imagined, but worse, to emotions he had no desire at all to feel. He was engulfed in tenderness, in passion, in the wildest intensities that he did not know whether to call pain or delight...and this on and on, while she, completely at ease, at home in her country, took him further and further every moment, a determined, but disquieted companion.

He could not of course sustain it for long. Equality is not learned in a lesson, or even two. He was heavy and slow in response by nature: he could never be anything else. Impossible to him would always be the quicksilver pleasures. But even as far as he could stand it, he had been introduced to his potentialities beyond anything he had believed possible. And when they desisted, and he was half relieved and half sorry that the intensities were over, she did not allow him to sink back again away from the plane of sensitivity they had both achieved. They made love all that night, and all the following day, and they did not stop at all for food, though they did ask for a little wine, and when they had been entirely and thoroughly wedded, so that they could no longer tell through touch where one began and the other ended, and had to look, with their eyes, to find out, they fell into a deep sleep, where they lay becalmed for another twenty-four hours. And when they woke, at the same moment, at the beginning of a nightfall, they heard a drum beat, beat, from the end of the garden, and this rhythm they knew at once was signalling to the whole land, and beyond it to her land, that the marriage was properly accomplished. And the drum was to beat, from that time on, from when they met, until they parted, so that everyone could know they were together, and share in the marriage, in thought, and in sympathetic support—and, of course, in emulation.

They lay in each other's arms as if in the shallows of a sea they had drowned in. But now began the slow and tactful withdrawals of the flesh, thigh from thigh, knee from knee. . .it was partly dark and while each felt their common-place selves to be at odds with the marvels of the days and nights just ended, luckily any dissonances could not be seen. For already they were quick to disbelieve what they had accomplished. He, with an apologetic and almost tender movement, pulled his warm forearm from under her neck, sat up, then stood up, stretching. Relief was in every stretch of those sturdy muscles, and she smiled in the dark. As for her, she was becoming herself again the same way. But it was clear he felt it was ungallant to leave her at once, for he pulled around himself his soldier's cloak and sat at the foot of the couch. . .

Doris Lessing
THE MARRIAGES BETWEEN ZONE
THREE, FOUR, AND FIVE

EXERCISES

1. Write of married love. Not the stress and the bickering and the money problems, but the sexual bonding between men and women. For the moment, leave out ideas about patriarchy, about inequality, about oppression. Concentrate on the physical attraction and energy possible between a man and a woman.

2. Visualize the man you would like to marry.

Henri Bergson theorizes that comedy arises when the natural becomes mechanical or when the mechanical begins to take on a life of its own. Certainly the latter provides the basis of humor in this poem. It would be hard to imagine a creature with more elan vital *than Doris the Robot.*

MODERN ROMANCE

One: The Wife

The reason
we got rid
of the robot
was
she was an
absolute slut.
You must
understand,
my Mortimor
is a strong
man
but how long
can even a good
man resist
temptation?
The way
she used to
look at him
and rub
against
him
every chance
she got. She
was a tramp,
that fancy
vacuum cleaner
with tits.

Two: The Husband

My wife never understood Doris.

I mean, the domestic robot.
She was a delight.
Intelligent yet submissive.
Sexy but didn't mind housework.
And she knew her place.
The perfect woman.
Must have been designed by a man.

Of course, a flesh and blood woman
is preferable to a machine
no
matter how perfect
and beautiful
and understanding
and responsive.

Poor Annie was so upset
by this
whole mess.
I think a vacation would do her
a world of good.
The Grand Canyon? That's the place. . .

Three: The Robot

Imagine me, marrying
a man like Mortimor.
Why this is the
happiest day of
my life & a true
advancement for
my people. I am
the first robot
in history
to marry a man
of Mortimor's stature.
Oh, he's so
brave to withstand
public opinion
and so strong
to

overcome that
tragedy
of last weekend
when his wife accidentally
fell to her death
from a great height
in Arizona.

William J. Harris
IN MY OWN DARK WAY

EXERCISES

1. Describe the perfect male robot. What tasks would he be capable of performing? Which functions would you leave out of his program? Ah, what an opportunity. . .

2. Describe the domestic robot Doris if she'd been designed by a woman—by the wife Annie, for instance.

SHOTGUN WEDDING

My sister found out she was pregnant, so she and her boyfriend decided to get married. Or so she said at the time. Later she told me that she'd gotten pregnant on purpose because (1) she wanted a baby and (2) she thought that he might be having an affair. When I told her that I thought this was manipulative, no way to start a marriage, etc., she just looked at me and shrugged. Then she picked up her baby and began to rock it. . . .

Since then, I've talked to several people who have also gotten pregnant on purpose or by being careless. "It's like I went into a dream state and sort of lost my diaphragm," one friend told me. Up until her biological alarm began to drown out all other sounds, this woman was a very together feminist. Now, she's all gaga over little booties and lace bibs. Her boyfriend is the type (selfish, narcissistic) who would never make a decision on his own—or a commitment. By her getting pregnant, this decision was made for him.

The thing is, both my sister and this friend seem very happy now. They aren't riddled with guilt or conscience over forcing a man to marry them or by reverting to what I see as very regressive female behavior. The real killer is that I have all these principles, but when they pick up their babies and cuddle them, I am eaten alive with jealousy.

Sylvia Kingston
Student

EXERCISES

1. Write a short play or story about a young, unmarried couple who find out that the woman is pregnant. What is her reaction? His? How does it change their relationship? You may wish to compare the unconscious, biological need the body has to reproduce (blindly, without considering human consequence) with the social movement of recent decades which urges a woman towards liberation, financial equality, and self-actualization. You may wish to try to find a metaphor to express the immensity of the evolutionary force (deep, dark sea; vast stretching deserts) and the relative size of our social movement (a minute floating chip; a single soon-to-be-swept-away grain). Then again, you may not.

2. Visualize yourself first as an unmarried woman who finds herself pregnant, then as her partner. Create a dialogue between the two.

CLOTHES

Scene 1

A department-store window, looking out on the street. MARCIA, a mannequin.

MARCIA

I am more beautiful than you. Yes I am. I know I am. I can see myself in
the glass. (Gaily) I went dancing at the Colony last night. Can't you tell? You
can tell by my dress. It's a Colony dancing dress and no one else has ever worn
it before. Oh, what a time we had! It was divine! It was madly gay! I danced
and danced and danced and danced—(Disappointed) Nobody's paying the
slightest attention. (She calls softly to the invisible crowd passing in front of
her window) Hello. . .Hi there. . .Ta... Ah-oo. . .(To herself) Of course I don't
mind. I don't mind at all. They'll turn the lights out soon, but if you think I
mind—!

I won't be able to see myself. I won't know who I am. I won't have any
memories, only the most awful nightmares, the most awful, awful—I don't
mind. One has to be brave. When they turn the lights out in the evening, you
can hear a little, sighing sound, like a hundred leaves all falling, all drifting and
circling down. That's all of us. We die, each time the lights are turned out. Of
course I don't mind. I just fix my eyes on a corner of the Park—I can see the
Park, you know, right over there—and when the sun comes up, that's the first
thing I see. I keep my eyes fixed on the fountain, on those trees. And that's the
first thing I see every morning. (Coaxing) You can see me. Of course you can.
Look at me. Look. No one's ever worn this dress before. Look how lovely my
shoes are. I have eyelashes. Look! Look at me! Please, please look at me!

(Enter IRVING, who stops, stares at her, awestruck. He bites his nails. He
scratches. Scruffy, grimy, badly dressed. Hunched over. She glows, poses,
yearns, leans towards him. He is fascinated. He rubs his hands together. Then
he jumps violently, as if stung, pulls his jacket closer around him and runs out.
The lights fade, MARCIA goes limp).

MARCIA

We die. . .We die. . .in the dark.

(The lights go out)

Scene 3

MARCIA, in the window, revolving slowly, talking, putting on and taking off items of clothing, etc. Scarves, hats, shawls. IRVING is staring off in front of her. A montage.

MARCIA

When you look at me, I feel as if someone were touching me.

IRVING

I work in a warehouse.

MARCIA

I feel something touching me and I can't bear it; it's so pleasant and so painful at once, I don't know what to do.

IRVING

You look rich.

MARCIA

I feel something like a fire, something going all through me, like a fire—

IRVING

You're a lady.

MARCIA

I don't know if I can stand it. I wonder if I want you to look at me at all.

IRVING

You're a real lady.

MARCIA

Look at me! I want you to look at me! (He does) Do you know what will happen to me? It happens to all of us. We get melted down or chopped up and we go back to being *things* and all the time we're *so* much more beautiful and *so* much more perfect than—than *real* women. . .(With dignity) Sometimes it occurs to me that I may end my days being used for land reclamation, but I don't cry—I never cry—(Stifling a sob) because—because—I know—I just look—over there—

IRVING

You! You're better than all of them.

MARCIA

No. Not really.

IRVING

You understand.

MARCIA

No. Not really.

IRVING

You love me.

MARCIA

No. Not really. (He kisses the window. She gasps) I love you!

(He rushes off. The WINDOW DESIGNER comes in and begins to take off her clothes as the lights fade out) . . .

> Joanna Russ
> "Window Dressing"
> THE NEW WOMEN'S THEATRE
> ed. Honor Moore

EXERCISES

1. Make an inventory of all of your clothes and shoes. Do not cheat. Well, maybe a little.

2. Describe your first (or most memorable) grown-up outfit. Recapture the scene surrounding buying (or making) it, who was involved, how it made you feel; write about wearing it for the first time.

3. Imagine yourself as a mannequin in a window. What are you wearing? What do people say about you? How does the inner you differ from their comments?

We're told that when Sylvia Plath read this poem aloud, she would laugh and laugh.

DADDY

You do not do, you do not do
Any more, black shoe
In which I have lived like a foot
For thirty years, poor and white,
Barely daring to breathe or Achoo.

Daddy, I have had to kill you.
You died before I had time—
Marble-heavy, a bag full of God,
Ghastly statue with one gray toe
Big as a Frisco seal

And a head in the freakish Atlantic
Where it pours bean green over blue
In the waters off beautiful Nauset.
I used to pray to recover you.
Ach, du.

In the German tongue, in the Polish town
Scraped flat by the roller
of wars, wars, wars.
But the name of the town is common.
My Polack friend

Says there are a dozen or two.
So I never could tell where you
Put your foot, your root,
I never could talk to you.
The tongue stuck in my jaw.

It stuck in a barb wire snare.
Ich, ich, ich, ich,
I could hardly speak
I thought every German was you.
And the language obscene

An engine, an engine
Chuffing me off like a Jew.
A Jew to Dachau, Auschwitz, Belsen.
I began to talk like a Jew.
I think I may well be a Jew.

The snows of the Tyrol, the clear beer of Vienna
Are not very pure or true.
With my gipsy ancestress and my weird luck
And my Taroc pack and my Taroc pack
I may be a bit of a Jew.

I have always been scared of you,
With your Luftwaffe, your gobbledygoo.
And your neat mustache
And your Aryan eye, bright blue.
Panzer-man, panzerman, O You—

Not God but a swastika
So black no sky could squeak through.
Every woman adores a Fascist,
The boot in the face, the brute
Brute heart of a brute like you.

You stand at the blackboard, daddy,
In the picture I have of you,
A cleft in your chin instead of your foot
But no less a devil for that, no not
Any less the black man who

Bit my pretty red heart in two.
I was ten when they buried you.
At twenty I tried to die
And get back, back, back to you.
I thought even the bones would do.

But they pulled me out of the sack,
And they stuck me together with glue.
And then I knew what to do.
I made a model of you,
A man in black with a Meinkampf look

And a love of the rack and the screw.
And I said I do, I do
So daddy, I'm finally through.
The black telephone's off at the root,
The voices just can't worm through.

If I've killed one man, I've killed two—
The vampire who said he was you
And drank my blood for a year,
Seven years, if you want to know.
Daddy, you can lie back now.

There's a stake in your fat black heart
And the villagers never liked you.
They are dancing and stamping on you.
They always *knew* it was you.
Daddy, daddy, you bastard, I'm through.

Sylvia Plath
ARIEL

EXERCISES

1. Write a poem about your father. As in the Plath poem, you may want to adopt a nursery rhyme rhythm to express deeper emotions. Or you may want to forget Plath altogether. Hold an image of your father in your mind (or look at a photograph), then write down what comes to you. One technique that sometimes produces strong results is to concentrate on an image or a photograph, but wait a full three minutes (set a kitchen timer) before you write a word. Try to keep your surface mind as blank as possible as you look at the image. Let the words come from "underneath."

2. Cluster on your father. Compare this clustering to the one you did on yourself (or do one on yourself if you haven't already. See CLUSTERING in Section One if you need assistance.) In what ways are you like him? Different?

3. Tell a story about your father that takes place before you were born.

FATHER

In the morning when I went to school, my father would put on his one good suit and his gray felt hat and ride down in the elevator with the other men on their way to the office. From the lobby he would walk down to the basement, to the windowless storage room that came with our apartment. That was where he worked. There, he hung up the suit and hat and wrote all morning in his boxer shorts, typing away on his portable Underwood set up on a folding table. At lunchtime he would put the suit back on and ride up in the elevator.

Susan Cheever
HOME BEFORE DARK: A Biographical
Memoir of John Cheever by his Daughter

EXERCISES

1. Concentrate on a particular habit of your father's and write about it. Pick a habit that implies something about his character.

2. Write a physical description of your father. Write as if you were looking at a video of him rather than a photograph.

3. Write a biography of your father. Make it as long and as complete as possible. If you find there are gaps, try to get the information from him or from people who know or knew him.

In the following passage, Daria, 42 years old, has been left by her husband of 22 years, Ross. Tracy is their daughter.

BREAKING UP

As soon as Tracy returned to college on January second, Daria felt the house swell around her, echoing like a church. As she tried to sleep, the house seethed with rustling, banging, muffled thuds. If she dozed, often she wakened in terror, sure an intruder stood over her bed.

Now for the first time, she was living alone. From the morning Ross had packed the set of matched leather luggage that had been a wedding present, she had given him up. She could not guess how he was changing and how he would further change, but she did not hope he would return. She grieved; she bled. Being deserted, discarded tore at her. She felt ugly, she felt used and used up. She did not, however, dream that Ross would return.

He had hurt her too deeply. He was no longer the man she loved. She had to understand him now not to love him better, to serve him better, but to be free at last of him. Their relationship was over, but not done with.

Because going to bed made her vulnerable to her fancies and fears, she retired late, to erode the long hours of darkness. Usually she was exhausted and managed to sleep. Then she woke between four and five every morning. Anxieties seemed suspended over her in a net that lowered instantly when she stirred. Finally she rose, ate a hasty breakfast and worked....Desolation settled over her like fine choking dust. How alone she was; how empty her life. She saw the years grey and dusty stretching ahead in which she was always isolated, in which she shrivelled slowly in her flesh and at last blew away on the wind.

Marge Piercy
FLY AWAY HOME

EXERCISES

1. Write about how you felt right after your divorce or the breakup of a significant relationship. Compare with the above passage from Marge Piercy's FLY AWAY HOME.

2. Describe your parents' divorce and its effect on you.

3. Imagine yourself married to—and subsequently divorced from—your current boyfriend.

DAILY COURAGE DOESNT COUNT

daily courage doesnt count
we don't get diplomas for it.
i worked hard for 5 years with one man,
then had 3 years graduate training with another.
but people called me a divorcee, & acted as if
i had done something wrong.
no one was happy for me,
no one gave me a coming out party.
but i tell you, i came out of those marriages
one smart bitch.

> alta
> I AM NOT A PRACTICING ANGEL

EXERCISES

1. Give yourself a degree and/or title that your earned in your marriage. PHT: "Putting Hubby Through" is an example; MAMA and RN also come to mind.

2. Visualize yourself and your life if you and/or your parents had never gotten a divorce.

DIVORCE

Eggs boiling in a pot.
They click
like castanets.
I put one in a cup
& slice its head off.

Under the wobbly egg white
is my first husband
Look how small he's grown
since we last met!

"Eat me," he says agreeably.
I hesitate, then bite.

The thick yolk runs down
my thighs.

I take another egg
& slice its head.
Inside is my second husband.
This one's better done.

"You liked the white," I say,
"I liked the yolk."

He doesn't speak
but scowls as if to say:
"Everyone always eats me
in the end."

I chew him up
but I spit out
his jet-black hair,
the porcelain jackets from his teeth,
his cufflinks, fillings,
eyeglass frames. . .

I drink my coffee
& I read the *Times.*

Another egg is boiling in the pot.

　　　　　　　　　Erica Jong
　　　　　　　　　HALF-LIVES

EXERCISES

1. Write a poem about divorce. Not a story, not a play. A poem. It can be your own divorce, your parents', a friend's, one you imagine, one you wish you'd gotten, or one you're glad you never went through with. But it has to be a poem.

2. Visualize your next husband in detail.

3. Visualize a former (or present) lover as he will be in 20 years.

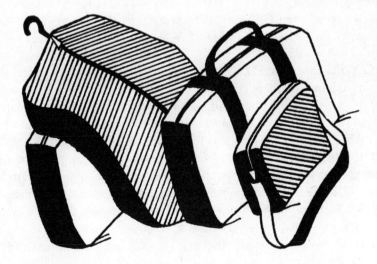

Therapist and author Daphne Rose Kingma suggests several writing exercises that lead to emotional healing while trying to get over an ended relationship. She advises that you provide a half hour to an hour of uninterrupted time for each one.

ENDING RELATIONSHIPS

EXERCISE ONE: The Love Story

When you get to the point of ending a relationship, you usually want to forget that you were ever in love in order to minimize the pain you feel now. But that's cheating. In order to really get over a relationship, you have to re-feel your way all the way through it, starting from the beginning, when you fell in love. After all, if you hadn't fallen in love, it wouldn't be so awful to fall out of love; if something hadn't captivated you originally, it wouldn't be so hard to let go now.

So rather than avoiding the memory which is the source of pain—and also of healing—begin by telling the story of your relationship:

A. Tell the story of how you fell in love. Include where you met, what attracted you, what there was about the other person which seemed to resonate with some deep wish or need of yours.

B. Tell a little bit about the early stages of your relationship, your first date, your first brief interlude together. Remember—and write—the feelings you had at that time, and also include your expectations. Because of your good feelings, you developed some expectations for this relationship. They were either conscious or unconscious; some of them were appropriate and were subsequently fulfilled, and some of them were way off the mark. Don't go into what finally occurred. Go back to the original time and the original feelings and write down the expectations you had. What did you expect would eventually occur in this relationship?

C. Write about what I call the "Clue of Failure." In every relationship, at the very beginning, there is a little clue that registers (and is subsequently disregarded) that something will go wrong eventually, that the relationship isn't going to last forever. It may be a very odd thing. One woman said, "I don't know why, but when I saw his tiny little bottom teeth, I knew it wouldn't work out." It turned out later that the man, who was physically immense, was, in fact, a very passive person, and it was his refusal to deal with his passivity which, in the end, caused their relationship to collapse. Somehow, at an unconscious level, her focusing on his little teeth was her awareness that he was not big, strong and powerful, but a very passive person.

Another woman said that the man she was breaking up with swore too much the first night they went out. He was very generous, attentive and appreciative of her, but as their relationship evolved she realized that his crude speech was an early indication of what later turned out to be an uncontrollable temper.

The point here is that there is always a clue—something which registers on a subliminal level and is subsequently disregarded, which is an indicator of what eventually occurs.

EXERCISE TWO: The Real Story

We all have a particular mythology we tell ourselves about every romance we get into. That's the "love story"—the story in which the original meeting is fated and magical, in which—we assume—that we will go on "living happily ever after."

The "love story" embodies the illusion, romance and hope part of any romantic relationship, whether or not that relationship eventually manages to be translated into a long-term life relationship.

As we have seen, by looking more closely at what is actually going on in our relationships, we discover that there is another reality which is simultaneously occurring—the developmental process. Exercise Two is designed to help you discover the developmental process that was operating in your relationship.

A. Write about what was going on in your life when your relationship began. What were you and your partner each trying to accomplish when you met? Were you starting a business, wanting to have children, trying to get a graduate degree?

B. Talk also about where you were in terms of relationship status. Were you waiting for a new relationship? Had you recently come out of a relationship? Were you in the middle of another love affair?

C. What was your developmental task? What was your partner's developmental task? Were you trying to get the good mothering you never had? Incorporate your sexuality? Gain a sense of your power, beauty or intelligence? Understand your father's unavailability, your mother's possessiveness?

D. What was your gift to him or her? What did he or she give you? An example: He helped me believe I was a lovable person and I rescued him from his mother's clutches.

E. How did the Clue of Failure ultimately manifest itself? For example, the person who had one too many drinks on the first date turned out to be an alcoholic. The person who didn't want to get together until next week turned out to be not available for a relationship. The person who was overly generous turned out to be a spendthrift.

F. If the story of your relationship was written up as a novel or made into a movie, what would it be called? Some examples: *Great Expectations; Two Ships That Should Have Passed in the Night; The Year of Living Dangerously; More is Less; Too Many Gin and Tonics.*

G. What was the *real* reason your relationship ended? This reason has to do with the completion of your developmental task. What task did you complete? What task did your partner complete? Some examples: "I outgrew my need for a mommy." "I finally got in touch with my power." "We finished raising the children." "It was all sex; that wasn't enough."

> Daphne Rose Kingma
> COMING APART: WHY RELATIONSHIPS
> END AND HOW TO LIVE THROUGH THE
> ENDING OF YOURS

EXERCISES

1. Write the "love story" of your ended relationship.

2. Write the real story, following the guidelines above.

STEPFAMILIES

After my parents' divorce, I used to spend the first weekend of every month with my father. I never talked much at his house. Never. He'd let me sit at his desk and play with his stuff. I always stole something: sheets of paper, thumbtacks, little things. I don't know why I did. When he'd go out to run, I'd go into his closet and smell his clothes. I don't know why I did that either, but I did.

Then my father married Jennifer. She tried to be nice to me, but she didn't know anything about kids. Pretty soon she gave it up (being nice to me). She wasn't un-nice so much as she just acted like I wasn't there. I didn't mind the weekends with them, but when I got home Mom wanted to know all about Jennifer. What kind of clothes did she have? Could she cook? Did she sleep late? All these dumb little things. After a while I started getting sick every time I was supposed to go to my father's for the weekend.

I'm never going to get married.

Student, University of California at Santa Barbara

EXERCISES

1. Write about stepfamilies.

2. Write about the ways your stepmother resembles/differs from your biological mother.

3. Create a story in which there is a positive and productive relationship between a stepmother and stepdaughter.

4. List some of the ways in which divorced parents make it difficult (economic and emotional blackmail, guilt, etc.) for their child to relate to the other parent or other family.

5. Describe your relationship to your stepmother from (1) your point of view (2) her point of view (3) your father's point of view and (4) an outsider's point of view. If appropriate, substitute stepchild for stepmother.

HIPS

One day you wake up and they are there. Ready and waiting like a new Buick with keys in the ignition. Ready to take you where?

They're good for holding a baby when you're cooking, Rachel says turning the jump rope a little quicker. She has no imagination.

You need them to dance, says Lucy.

If you don't get them you may turn into a man. Nenny says this and she believes it. She is this way because of her age.

That's right, I add before Lucy or Rachel can make fun of her. She is stupid alright, but she is my sister.

But most important, hips are scientific, I say repeating what Alicia already told me. It's the bones that let you know which skeleton was a man's when it was a man and which a woman's.

They bloom like roses, I continue because it's obvious I'm the only one that can speak with any authority; I have science on my side. The bones just one day open. Just like that. One day you might decide to have kids, and then where are you going to put them? Got to have room. Bones got to give.

But don't have too many or your behind will spread. That's how it is, says Rachel whose mama is as wide as a boat. And we just laugh.

What I'm saying is who here is ready? You gotta be able to know what to do with hips when you get them, I say making it up as I go. You gotta know how to walk with hips, practice you know—like if half of you wanted to go one way and the other half the other.

Sandra Cisneros
THE HOUSE ON MANGO STREET

EXERCISES

1. Write for 20 minutes about a part of your body. Pick a part that you like—your hands, for instance. Try to think of a metaphor which visually expresses something about them as Cisneros does with hips.

2. Pick a part of your body that you don't like—your feet, say—and try to express what you don't like about them, how life could have been different if only they'd been different. Many of my students write about their breasts in this context, usually about breasts that are too small or too big, but occasionally just right.

PENIS

The little naked boy walks about the village, his steps uncertain, his balance precarious. When he slips, his hand goes to his penis, to keep his balance. Or after he has tripped, his hand goes to his penis as if assuring himself that it is still there, and also to clutch for support. There are no blind spots in the language that prevent any one's calling his penis by any name at all, or which devalue it and make it seem to vanish away, as can happen in language in which prudery has robbed the human tongue of any words for the organs of procreation or the acts of procreation—usually through an unfortunate over-association with acts of excretion. People speak to him of his penis as they do of his arms or legs, his eyes or nose. It is something that he has, indubitably, definitely. He is male. He is small, but some day by the steps he sees represented by the growing boys about him he will be adult. He will be a man and not a woman.

Margaret Mead
MALE AND FEMALE

EXERCISES

1. Write about a penis, being aware of linguistic blind spots and cultural prudery.

2. Visualize yourself as a man.

These two passages are excerpted from women students' papers.

WORDS

One day I was walking downtown and happened to catch the eye of a street person, a young but ratty looking man. I try not to look at them in the eye because they ask you for money and he did, but I kept walking: "Ma'am, can you spare some change." Then he kept calling "Ma'am, ma'am." When I kept walking, he called out, "Cunt, don't got no change, huh Cunt." From ma'am to cunt in about 20 feet. It made me feel dirty, but also very trapped. What could I do? Turn around on Main Street and call him, "Prick."?

***

I went into a bar one time and this bartender came up and said, "What'll it be, honey." I don't know why I liked it so much, but I did. Maybe it made me feel pretty or loved or something, but I really liked it when he called me that. I'm not the type that people usually call honey so I guess that is why I liked it. It sort of made my day.

EXERCISES

1. Describe an event in which one of the above words was used on you and its effect.

2. Make a list of all the words you can think of that are used to denote "female." All.

3. Make a list of all of the names used for "male." Compare your two lists.

SEXY

Hannah simply refused to live without the attentions of a man, and after Rekus' death had a steady sequence of lovers, mostly the husbands of her friends and neighbors. Her flirting was sweet, low and guileless. Without ever a pat of the hair, a rush to change clothes or a quick application of paint, with no gesture whatsoever, she rippled with sex. In her same old print wraparound, barefoot in the summer, in the winter her feet in a man's leather slippers with the backs flattened under her heels, she made men aware of her behind, her slim ankles, the dew-smooth skin and the incredible length of neck. Then the smile —eyes, the turn of the head—all so welcoming, light and playful. Her voice trailed, dipped and bowed; she gave a chord to the simplest words. Nobody, but nobody, could say "hey sugar" like Hannah. When he heard it, the man tipped his hat down a little over his eyes, hoisted his trousers and thought about the hollow place at the base of her neck. And all this without the slightest confusion about work and responsibilities. While Eva tested and argued with her men, leaving them feeling as though they had been in combat with a worthy, if amiable, foe, Hannah rubbed no edges, made no demands, made the man feel as though he were complete and wonderful just as he was—he didn't need fixing—and so he relaxed and swooned in the Hannah-light that shone on him simply because he was. If the man entered and Hannah was carrying a coal scuttle up from the basement, she handled it in such a way that it became a gesture of love. He made no move to help her with it simply because he wanted to see how her thighs looked when she bent to put it down, knowing that she wanted him to see them too.

But since in that crowded house there were no places for private and spontaneous lovemaking, Hannah would take the man down into the cellar in the summer where is was cool behind the coal bin and the newspapers, or in the winter they would step into the pantry and stand up against the shelves she had filled with canned goods, or lie on the flour sack just under the rows of tiny green peppers. When those places were not available, she would slip into the seldom-used parlour, or even up to her bedroom. She liked the last place least, not because Sula slept in the room with her but because her love mate's tendency was always to fall asleep afterwards and Hannah was fastidious about whom she slept with. She would fuck practically anything, but sleeping with someone implied for her a measure of trust and a definite commitment. . . .

Toni Morrison
SULA

EXERCISES

1. Write a short sketch of the sexiest, most man-oriented woman you have ever known. What makes her sexy?

2. What is a sexy woman's effect on the men around her? On women?

COMING OUT

I didn't mean to come out. More like I was pushed. Shoved. It happened in a revival tent in North Carolina. I was 15, we were both 15. Her father was the preacher. Mean as a snake, mean to her, mean to everyone. But still the preacher. We'd been in this tent all night, everyone talking about their sins, crying and carrying on. My parents were glad that I'd come with them. I usually didn't like to go to revivals and they didn't make me. Tonight, I'd come because I wanted to see her. She was the first person I'd ever loved. I wanted it to be forever.

Then she got up and said she'd sinned. I nearly died. I knew what was coming. I tried to signal to her, but she wouldn't look at me. She was crying. "What sin?" her father asked.

"A sin with another girl." The audience gasped.

"Name this girl that led you to the devil."

She shook her head.

But he kept on and on. "Name her. Name her. You can't be forgiven until you've told us her name." She held out for a while but then her father worked it around that the other girl was the devil and had tricked her. I think she believed him. She stood up and pointed her finger at me. I felt my parents go rigid on either side of me.

But that wasn't enough. "Say her name, say her name and renounce the devil," her father told her. "It is the only way to be forgiven of your sin and come back into the fold."

"Jane Woodard," she said it soft, but without love. I ran out of the tent before the preacher could start in on me.

That's how I came out.

Student,
University of California at Santa Barbara

EXERCISES

1. Write a short sketch in the third person of someone coming out of the closet as a homosexual. You may want to think of someone you know and imagine the process that they went through. Or, if you are gay, tell your own story in the first person.

2. Now write the same sketch in the first person.

CONSTANT INTERRUPTUS

(Writing erotica at home, especially on a weekend, is a test of sexual prowess, for it requires the same intensity of focus as an actual sex act. Since I am often easily distracted during lovemaking at home, writing erotica in broad daylight without any locks on the doors helps to increase my staying power. It also may explain why so many of my stories are short.)

Our attraction ionized the air as palpably as lightning about to strike.
First son: Hey, Mom! Today's the day I'm gonna get a parrot! Can you give me a ride?
The passion that danced in the wings of my daydreams was about to take centerstage. Caught by
Daughter: Why doesn't the dishwasher go on?
his unswerving gaze, I watched him dodge the other passengers as he hurtled after me to the back of the car. I was afraid our urgency would set off emergency alarms, and I nervously scanned the faces of the rush-hour commuters,
Husband: I need the 1984 tax returns right away.
who continued to stare impassively ahead, resigned to their fates and oblivious to ours.
The train pulled away from the station with a lurch, so overloaded was it with the weight of our desire. Trembling with mounting speed, it lumbered towards the dark shaft
Daughter: There's no water pressure.
of the tunnel.
Every seat was taken, but we found room enough to stand together at the rear of the car. Trenchcoated veterans surrounded us, hemming us in behind a wall of khaki. Secure in our pocket of privacy, I tore open
DOORBELL
Workman: Pardon me, ma'am, but there seems to be a leak in the water main. Do you have a wrench?
my coat, and we pressed even closer. I could feel his exhalations coming in humid puffs in my hair just as the hot breath of a passing train blasted the window to my back. With one deft movement he lifted my sweater and unclasped
TELEPHONE
Friend: Oh, I'm so glad you're there. I really need to talk. Martin has just moved out.
my bra. His kisses began to rain down upon
Second son: I need wrapping paper. Where is it?
my bare breasts

Second son: Which closet?
"Oh, God. Oh, God," I moaned,
Second son: Where did you say?
as he gently traced
Second son: Now where's the present?
each areola
Husband: Did you want to leave those potatoes burning?
with his tongue. The liquid proof of my desire
Daughter: May I wear your black pants tonight?
dissolved all sense of time and place, deafened us to the song of steel rails, and blinded us to the streaking lights that flashed past.
Husband: You forgot to list the charitable contributions.
We clung to each other, clenched more tightly than a fist, holding our
DOORBELL
Workman: Ma'am, the valve is rusted so bad I can't get it to turn. You'll have to get someone from the water department out here right away.
breath, until the pressure became unbearable, and we
TELEPHONE
Mother-in-law: Hello, Rose. What are you doing today?
Rose: Oh, nothing much.

> Rose Solomon
> LOOK HOMEWARD EROTICA
> Kensington Ladies' Erotica Society

EXERCISES

1. Write about trying to write at home.

2. Compare erotica with actual sexual experience.

SHOWING TEDDY

"There are some rules," I said. We both stared at one another. This was serious.

Teddy was the other half of my kindergarten carpool. We were at the side of my house, cleverly concealed by the thick, green foliage.

"Number one, you promise never to tell. Number two, don't touch anything. And number three, don't put anything in it, like a twig, or a rock."

He nodded, and he waited.

"Lay on the ground," I instructed. I took off my pants and stood over him. We were silent for a long time. Finally he commented, "I can't see much."

"Most of it is inside. You can't see the really important stuff." I pulled back on my pants and explained, mimicking what I had been taught, "All of the special body parts inside of me will someday form a baby. Girls are lucky enough, and special enough, to have these parts. Your parts are important too, but my parts are *really* important for the baby to grow and live."

At this point, Teddy wasn't listening. He was walking back to the swingset and climbing up the ladder to the slide.

"I can tell you more about this later," I said, "Just ask." I went across the yard, sat on a swing, and joined him.

Debbie Boehm, Student,
University of California at Santa Barbara

EXERCISES

1. To whom did you show what? Describe the experience. What happened? Were there consequences? What message did you get about sexuality from the experience?

2. Visualize Teddy. Experience his reaction to being shown.

CHILD'S PLAY

By the time I was ten, Lisa and I had developed a game which we played whenever we were together. It was a "touch game" which really required going to bed together. This was conveniently arranged by setting up sleepover dates at one another's houses, dates on which we pleaded to sleep together in order to talk after the lights were out. After our parents had knocked on the door at least three or four times, telling us to be quiet (we disobeyed the order deliberately, not wanting to seem too obedient and cause suspicion), we got down to the really important business of the evening. We lay there with our arms around each other, kissing each other's flat chests, turned upside down to nuzzle at each other, used our tongues, and even went so far as to imitate the dogs we had seen on the street by crawling around and around the bed sniffing one another. We giggled a great deal in between our exploits, half from nervousness and half from sheer sensual pleasure. Then deep in the darkness, we murmured dirty jokes in one another's ears... relishing especially the one about the Exploring Fly which was so graphic that it never ceased to inspire us.

Lisa and I, of course, had no "ideas" about what we were doing. We knew, though, that it would be bad if we were caught. We considered grownups to be too proper for such things and expected that they would never understand how fine it was to lie together feeling such intense and joyous animal pleasure from touching one another. If, in all likelihood, they would think we were terrible, then the only solution was not to let them know, to protect their innocence and make sure that we would have the freedom to continue our explorations. (It is in this way, I suppose, that parents and children mutually reinforce the myths about each other's naivete, which can never be substantiated, since neither ever dares to raise the questions that would shatter forever the dimly romanticized aura that surrounds the other, and preserves the desired distance between them.)

I certainly had never stopped doing anything because I was told it was bad. But if I had actually been caught fooling around with Lisa I am sure I would have cried for shame, not over the act itself, but over the violation of my world which discovery implied, since what I really felt I had to protect was my sense perceptions against the onslaught of values that were denied by everything I had experienced. Those values, however, were extraordinarily insidious, so that even as I was denying that I cared what my parents thought, I soon started having nightmarish fantasies about becoming sterile for the rest of my life as a result of what I considered to be my "perversion." In my dreams, I was constantly being tortured and tossed into pits. I was a lesbian, I thought. The most terrible thing one could possibly be. Being a lesbian meant one thing to me. . . not doing what we had done, but having people look at you as if you had just decided to shit in the middle of their expensive living room rug. Lesbianism was not what one did; it was what people thought about what one did. And that was bad. Very bad. Not only bad...it was disgusting.

> Ingrid Bengis
> COMBAT IN THE EROGENOUS ZONE:
> Writings on Love, Hate and Sex

EXERCISES

1. Rewrite the above incident from the narrator's mother's point of view.

2. Write for 20 minutes about sexual guilt.

3. Describe your sex play as a child. If you wish, use the third person rather than the first.

4. Write for 20 minutes on lesbianism.

5. Write a short story about a woman who makes love to another woman for the first time.

NOON

Noon, there's never any place to park.
But there was one
Way back, waiting.

Noon, she had just an hour
Before her exam.
But she was ready.

And he was there.
All at once.
No chance to prepare.

He told her he wouldn't hurt her.
But it hurt.
The gravel dug into her knees.

How long did it take this way?

Kneeling there,
She thought of the things she had to do:
Her exam, turn in her paper,
Lunch with Gail.

Would they give her an incomplete now?

Should never have taken that space.
Too far away,
Near those bushes,
Hidden.

But noon, there's never any place to park.
You can't pick and choose.
You're lucky to get anything.

And it was waiting.

Sarah Fenstermaker
Chair, Women's Studies Program,
University of California at Santa Barbara

EXERCISES

1. Express the emotions that are in abeyance or repressed in this poem.

2. Think about the ways you modify your behavior every day because of the existence of rapists in the world.

3. Imagine the long term effects on a woman.

DATE RAPE PREVENTION

Date or acquaintance rape means being forced or pressured into having sex by someone you know—against your will, without your consent.

1. Know that it could happen to you: studies at colleges indicate that between ten to 25 percent of women report they were raped by men they knew.

2. Be assertive in setting boundaries for relationships. Even casual unwanted contact should be firmly discouraged. It is easier to fight off a big attack if you've practiced on smaller intrusions.

3. Judge a person by his *behavior*, not his race, looks, socio-economic status, or even his relationship to you. Watch out for someone who:
- gets hostile when you say "no"
- ignores your wishes, opinions, ideas
- attempts to make you feel guilty or accuse you or being uptight if you say "no" to sex
- acts excessively jealous or possessive; keeps tabs on your whereabouts
- displays destructive anger and aggression

4. Define your limits, ie, how much touch you want with different male friends (handshake, kiss on cheek, kiss on mouth, hug with both arms, intercourse, no touch). Think about this in advance, even though you can change your mind later.

5. Defend your limits: "I don't like it when you do that"; "I like you and I don't want to do to bed with you"; "Let's go to the coffeehouse (instead of around the lagoon)." You have the right to be respected, to change your mind, to say "no" or just say, "Because I don't want to." Practice saying "no" clearly —don't hint, don't expect anyone to read your mind.

6. Be prepared for his reaction to your defending your limits. Possible reactions include hostility, embarrassment, blaming you for leading him on. *You are not responsible for his behavior or his reaction*; if he is someone you care about, you may wish to help him through the embarrassment, but you do not need to feel responsible. You have every right to your own decisions.

7. Most date rapes involve men and women who conform to traditional, rigid sex roles so it is important to examine sexism in order to prevent rape.

Avoid stereotypes such as "anger is unfeminine" that prevent you from expressing yourself.

8. Be aware of situations when you do not feel relaxed and in charge. Stereotypes of passivity, coyness, and submissiveness can contribute to a climate for male aggression—which is *his* stereotype.

9. Communicate clearly! Say "no" when you mean no; "yes" when you mean yes; stay in touch with your feelings to know the difference.

10. Believe and act as if you come first, without exploiting others. Treat yourself and others with respect.

Cheri Gurse

EXERCISE

1. Describe how reading the above makes you feel.

2. List the ways in which traditional male and female roles contribute to date rape.

THE KIWI BIRD

(A bird in New Zealand
that's forgotten how to fly)

I am the Kiwi bird
the one without wings. . .
Don't speak to me.
Don't call me.
I don't understand you. . .
Because I can't fly
And because some children
throw stones at me
I've become dull.
My beak opens sometimes, by itself
as if I were thirsty,
as if I were sick,
but I'm neither thirsty nor sick,
I am only dull
very, very dull.
Other times however
I think I hear something,
something like a flapping of sheets in the wind,
of wings in flight,
and then I walk a little,
I raise my stiff legs,
and my steps seem suddenly alert—
but I immediately sit down on the ground
and with my long beak,
I begin to scratch my wingless back
as if there were nothing left in the world
but me and my beak that pokes.
I am the Kiwi bird, the one that can't comprehend.
Don't speak to me.
Don't call me.
Once every few years, it happens,
when the moon seems to hum, to ring in a certain way
that shame and sorrow, my only emotions
start glimmering in my flesh,
and then I want to hide
I have nowhere

and I bend and twist,
And I have nothing with which to cover myself.

I am the Kiwi bird
the one without wings.
I am the Kiwi bird.

Nina Cassian
LADY OF MIRACLES,
Poems by Nina Cassian, Selected and Translated
from the Romanian by Laura Schiff

EXERCISES

1. Remember the eagle, dove, vulture, canary, wren, condor, parrot, love bird, ostrich, hawk, peacock, albatross, chicken, and turkey. Decide which kind of bird you are and write a poem expressing yourself as that bird.

2. Visualize the people in your life as different types of birds.

This selection is the first page of a story titled "Unguided Tour" to be found in the collection I, ETCETERA.

PLACE

I took a trip to see the beautiful things. Change of scenery. Change of heart. And do you know?

What?

They're still there.

Ah, but they won't be there for long.

I know. That's why I went. To say goodbye. Whenever I travel, it's always to say goodbye.

The roofs, timbered balconies, fish in the bay, the copper clock, shawls drying on the rocks, the delicate odor of olives, sunsets behind the bridge, ocher stone. "Gardens, parks, forests, woods, canals, private lakes, with huts, villas, gates, garden seats, gazebos, alcoves, banqueting houses, rotundas, observatories, aviaries, greenhouses, icehouses, fountains, bridges, boats, cascades, baths." The Roman amphitheater, the Etruscan sarcophagus. The monument to the 1914-1918 war dead in every village square. You don't see the military base. It's out of town, and not on the main road.

Omens. The cloister wall has sprung a long diagonal crack. The water level is rising. The marble saint's nose is no longer aquiline.

This spot. Some piety always brings me back to this spot. I think of all the people who were here. Their names scratched into the bottom of the fresco.

Vandals!

Yes. Their way of being here.

Susan Sontag
I, ETCETERA

EXERCISES

1. Describe a place. Try to be as specific and concrete as possible in order to convey the atmosphere of a location. Recreate sounds and smells as well as sights.

2. Remember a place from your past. As you write about it, let the memories flow.

3. Write a short story with a strong sense of place. Let the setting itself become, in effect, a character in the story.

4. Write of a place that holds terror, perhaps evil. Describe it in specific detail.

5. Describe your house, not as it is, but as you would like it to be.

FEAR

In the middle of the night silence wakes me, the rain has stopped. Blank dark, I can see nothing, I try to move my hands but I can't. The fear arrives like waves, like footfalls, it has no center; it encloses me like armor, it's my skin that is afraid, rigid. They want to get in, they want me to open the windows, the door, they can't do it by themselves. I'm the only one, they are depending on me but I don't know any longer who they are; however they come back they won't be the same, they will have changed. I willed it, I called to them, that they should arrive is logical; but logic is a wall, I built it, on the other side is terror.

Above on the roof is the finger-tapping of water dripping from the trees. I hear breathing, withheld, observant, not in the house but all around it.

Margaret Atwood
SURFACING

EXERCISES

1. Recreate a situation in which you were afraid. Try to feel the fear fully and to recreate its emotional intensity as you write.

2. Make a list of things you fear most.

3. Make a list of things you used to fear and now don't.

4. Go over your first list and decide which fears can or will be gotten over in time. Describe the process you will use to alleviate the fear, and the effect the lack of this fear is likely to have on your life.

5. Describe a chronic fear and the effect it has had on your life. Give the fear a name and enter into a dialogue with it.

6. There is generalized fear in the world. Try to articulate this fear.

7. Visualize your fears—large and small—see them as animals, insects, funny looking creatures from the deep. Dispose of them, make friends with them, feed them and let them go.

8. Imagine yourself as a small, furry animal on a hillside at night. Express this experience in a poem.

9. List ten ways in which you deal with fear or have dealt with it in the past.

10. Take 20 deep breaths as you visualize your fears, then write for 20 minutes without stopping on whatever comes into your mind.

Simone de Beauvoir is the author of THE SECOND SEX, a seminal work on feminism. This excerpt is from the first volume of her autobiography.

SISTERHOOD

I was glad, too, that I was not entirely at the mercy of grown-ups; I was not alone in my children's world; I had an equal: my sister, who began to play a considerable role in my life about my sixth birthday. . .

I owe a great debt to my sister for helping me to externalize many of my dreams in play: she also helped me to rescue my daily life from silence; through her I got into the habit of wanting to communicate with people. When she was not there I hovered between two extremes: words were either insignificant noises which I made with my mouth, or whenever I addressed my parents, they became deeds of the utmost gravity; but when Poupette and I talked together, words had a meaning yet did not weigh heavily upon us. I never knew with her the pleasure of sharing or exchanging things, because we always held everything in common; but as we recounted to one another the day's incidents and emotions, they took on added interest and importance. There was nothing wrong in what we told each other; nevertheless, because of the importance we both attached to our conversations, they created a bond between us which isolated us from the grown-ups; when we were together, we had our own secret garden.

Simone de Beauvoir
MEMOIRS OF A DUTIFUL DAUGHTER

EXERCISES

1. Write about your sister.

2. Write about the power and difficulty of all types of sisterhood, biological and ideological. Consider what degree of expectation you bring to a "sisterly" relationship.

THE LUST FOR MURDER

and the undecided question
why didn't i do it
(sometimes wisely thinking
good thing I didn't
and yet. . .
and yet sometimes i admit
the clean finality of murder
appeals to my aesthetic
sensibility the very thought
of it satisfies my soul
the way legal
arrangements do not)
times i want a knife
in my hand
a stone dagger
and i will be a priestess
and he will lie on the operating
table and i will bring
my hand down from where
it was fully raised in the air
and i will make an incision
in his chest
and with my hand
remove his red beating heart
and raise it up while
the blood flows down
my arm over my white robes
and then
i will feed it to
the lowest of the animals
that's what i wanted
not what happened in
the courtroom where i signed
my name to the pages
of papers and it was all
over and my left hand had to
hold the right hand by the wrist
so that it would be steady
enough to sign

oh no it was not a pen
i wanted in my hand

　　　Gerda Penfold
　　　DONE WITH MIRRORS

EXERCISES

1. Write out your anger at someone in the strongest possible terms.

2. Transform your anger: watch your anger as it rises, watch it twist and turn, watch it slip back into your mind. Now write about it again.

DYNAMICS OF WHO PICKS UP THE TAB

"I've always had pretty good relationships with women, both as friends and in the romantic sense," Rick writes. "Maybe it's because I try to treat them as equals. I have just one question. If the equal rights amendment ever passes, do you think it will occur to a woman someday that it's her turn to pick up a restaurant check?

"She may be making as much money as I do, this particular restaurant may even be her idea, all her senses may be finely tuned to any hint of 'sexism' on my part, but when the check comes she is suddenly seized with a fit of blindness. The man is afraid to suggest sharing because he doesn't want to look cheap."

Ah, that touches a tender spot for a lot of males. What is this strange reluctance to open the purse if she can afford to? Equal rights surely mean equal responsibility. In today's world why should he alone always pay for the privilege of her company?

Rick, the woman's movement is still only half a generation old, and a great many females simply haven't joined up. They accept the advances already won but see no reason on the personal level to challenge old familiar and safe attitudes.

A traditional woman would no more think of "paying a check for a man" than her mother would. You are right: She is blind because the possibility simply does not enter her head.

Other women have had their consciousness raised but deep in the heart do not believe that the scale balances between the sexes. Everything still tilts in the male direction. Sharing a check may seem vaguely like a fair idea in a perfect world; but right now it ranks No. 32 in her list of priorities.

Women have always been poor. If they worked at all, it was at subsistence jobs that rarely allowed the luxury of "eating out." Even when a woman moves up to a well-paying career she may still feel uneasy about spending a lot of money on restaurants.

She'll pay for clothes or travel or theater tickets, but fancy restaurants all too often come off as another male vanity, an effort to impress her. If so, that's his hang-up, and let him pay for it.

Every woman has also encountered a number of Good Ol' Boys who would gallantly break her arm before they'd let her touch a check. A business woman can invite a customer to lunch. He listens to her sales pitch and knows her company is picking up the tab, but he still plops his credit card down on top of hers. Wouldn't feel right treating a Little Lady any other way.

If there's one thing a woman doesn't want to do these days, it's make a man feel uncomfortable, to look pushy in seeming to question a traditional source of male status—his ability to pay for a meal. How open have you been in discussing your feelings about reciprocity? A woman instinctively looks to a man to define the terms of the relationship he is seeking.

Ideally, nobody should get involved in heavy dating expenses until some kind of tentative friendship has had time to bud. Then he smiles and asks, "Are you buying me a cup of coffee today?" It's a simple and honest way to present the idea of "sharing."

Women always respond to a man who opens up. If you are really hard-pressed financially, it's a rare woman who can't think of a dozen ways you can be together without spending a lot.

If money is not the issue, but you'd like her to make an occasional symbolic gesture of sharing, say so. But understand that her reciprocity is likely to be of a different kind. How much value, for example, do you put on a home-cooked dinner she's slaved over for three days in advance?

Lots of men really don't want to surrender control in dating situations, but that's what equality is about. Women enjoy being entertained in the grand style, of course, but generally they don't require it. What they do need is honest communication about how a man really thinks and feels.

If he's slow in that department, ladies, why don't you just offer to take him out to lunch—and see what happens?

> Jim Sanderson
> "Liberated Male" column,
> LOS ANGELES TIMES, September 26, 1984

EXERCISES

1. Answer Rick's letter yourself.

2. Write a short character sketch of Rick, including something on his background and his relationship with women.

3. Create a dialogue between a "liberated" male and "liberated" female concerning a restaurant check.

4. What is your response to this article? Do you feel it has hidden sexist undertones? Defend your position in writing.

WAGE GAP

Women earn 64 cents for each dollar earned by a man.

In 1984, the median earnings of women working full time year round was
$14,479 while the median earnings of men working full time year round was
$23,218.

A woman with four years of college earns less than a male high school dropout.

> Bureau of the Census
> August 1985

EXERCISES

1. Describe how the above statistics make you feel.

2. List what you plan to do about it.

3. Write a short history of your relationship with the workplace; how it would
have been different had you been a man; and what it will be like in the future.

MATERNITY LEAVE

Gail Tobias is a writer. For the last six years she has been one of the principal writers for a TV soap opera. In late 1983, at the age of thirty-five, Gail became pregnant with her first child. Gail's employer had no provisions for maternity leave in place, and so after extensive negotiation it was arranged that Gail should work right up to when she went into labor and then take two and a half weeks off for the delivery. One and a half weeks of this comprised Gail's paid vacation time; the other week was defined as leave at half pay. In the event, Gail had a difficult labor and eventually delivered her child by cesarean section. She therefore found it particularly difficult to be back on the job so soon after the birth. In Gail's words, "I don't know how I lived through those first weeks back at work. I was exhausted and in pain from the surgery. I could hardly drag myself around. The worse thing was the lack of sleep. Annie woke to be fed at least three times a night, and by midday I was ready to kill for sleep. But somehow I had to work—to smile and pretend to my boss that I didn't have a family care in the world." Gail is convinced that she would have lost her job had she taken additional time off. "I'm in a very competitive field, and they would have filled my slot easily and quickly." Since she and her husband have recently bought a house, they could not manage without her salary. Gail's poor maternity coverage extended to medical costs. She estimates that $1,800 of the childbirth expenses were not covered by medical insurance.

The experiences of many European women I interviewed throw Gail's struggle into sharp relief. Take Susan Arnbom who works as a secretary in Stockholm and has three children, ages eight, three, and two. When each of her children was born, Susan was entitled to nine months' paid leave at 90 percent of her salary plus a six-month job protected, but unpaid, leave. Since her two youngest children were born within a year of each other, she chose to merge her maternity leaves into a consecutive two-and-one-half year period. Her husband was also eligible to share parental leave with her, and he took a four-month leave at the time of the birth of their first child.

Sylvia Ann Hewlett
A LESSER LIFE: THE MYTH OF WOMEN'S
LIBERATION IN AMERICA

EXERCISES

1. Write a letter to your Congressperson advocating guaranteed paid maternity leave for all women in America. Mail it.

2. Imagine a world where the birthing and raising of children is incorporated into the very structure of job situation.

FEMINISM

In March of 1987, the University of Southern California hosted a conference called "Ecofeminist Perspectives." The flyer reads: ". . . what we propose is a conference that will critically examine an emerging perspective known as "ecofeminism" that links the exploitation of the Earth with the subordination of women. . . ."

EXERCISE

1. List and define several types of feminism besides "ecofeminism"; for example, "econofeminism" would be an obvious choice since women make 64 cents for every dollar made by a man.

STUDENT SAMPLE

"How about defining feminism in terms of the chakras or centers of energy up and down the spinal cord? The first or root chakra has to do with all the animal or unconscious functions, so we'll start with the second or sexual chakra. God knows there could be books written about Second Chakra Feminism. (Did you say this was a 20 minute exercise?) There's abortion, reproduction, sexual choice, male and female relationships, sex, birth control. I'll come back to this one.

The third chakra is the power chakra and it seems to me that feminism itself comes out of this chakra—the assertion of women against being passive and defined by others. The whole patriarchal power system springs from this one in the men and is answered by feminism. Then there is the manipulative power that women have traditionally exerted. . .

The fourth chakra is the heart chakra, associated with love and emotion. Fourth chakra feminism would insist on men learning to love and live in harmony with nature. Ecofeminism would be fourth chakra feminism in a way. The sort of maternal approach to the world that Dorothy Dinerstein talks about in *The Mermaid and the Minotaur* would come in here.

The fifth chakra is associated with the throat or with speech. Fifth chakra feminism would be the articulation of all the issues, the political argument. The ability to speak.

The sixth chakra is also the third eye, the vision. This is where the women like Lynn Andrew's Agnes Whistling Elk and other Spirit women merge with feminism. Women seeing into another world, seeing another reality. Very different from Second Chakra stuff.

The last center of energy is the crown chakra which connects with the spiritual world. This would be where the goddess comes in, the female principle. It is more mythic than the third eye, more cosmic, although the two are connected. A whole set of feminists talk about the Great Goddess and the spiritual aspects of being female, but it seems to me that this chakra would exist beyond any conception of male or female, thus beyond feminism. Maybe all of the spiritual stuff should go into the third eye chakra and let the crown chakra remain the one where we finally leave feminism (and the need for it) behind.

GENDER

Outside industrial societies, unisex work is the rare exception, if it exists at all. Few things can be done by women and also by men. The latter, as a rule, just cannot do women's work. In early eighteenth-century Paris, you could recognize the bachelor from afar by his stench and gloomy looks. From notaries' records, we know that solitary men left no sheets or shirts when they died. In the time of Louis XIV, a man without a woman to keep house could barely survive. Without wife, sister, mother, or daughter he had no way to make, wash, and mend his clothes; it was impossible for him to keep chickens or to milk a goat: if he was poor, he could not eat butter, milk, or eggs. He could not cook certain foods even if he had the ingredients. And today, in the rural Mexico I know so well, a woman would rather die of embarrassment than let a man cook the beans.

From afar, the native can tell whether women or men are at work, even if he cannot distinguish their figures. The time of year and day, the crop, and the tools reveal to him who they are. Whether they carry a load on their head or shoulder will tell him their gender. If he notices geese loose in the harvested field, he knows a girl must be nearby to tend them. If he comes across sheep, he knows he will find a boy. To *belong* means to know what befits *our* kind of woman, *our* kind of man. If someone does what *we* consider the other gender's work, that person must be a stranger. Or a slave, deprived of all dignity. Gender is in every step, in every gesture, not just between the legs. Puerto Rico is only three hours from New York. Two-thirds of its people have been to the mainland. Yet even today, in the interior of the island, there is no such thing as a Puerto Rican gait; woman sail down a path like sloops chopping in the tradewinds, and men swagger and roll to the rhythm of the machete, but both in the unmistakably *jibaro* fashion. One knows that they could not be from nearby Santo Domingo, much less be gringos from the States. In many Puerto Ricans, vernacular gender has survived for decades, not only in the Harlem barrio but even when they have lived mixed up with hillbillies and blacks in the South Bronx.

Gender is something other and much more than sex. It bespeaks a social polarity that is fundamental and in no two places the same. What a man cannot or must do is different from valley to valley. But the social anthropologist has missed the point, and his terminology has become a unisex mask for a reality that has two sides. What Bohr and Heisenberg have done for the epistemology of physics has not yet been done for the social sciences. That light fits the paradigms of both particle and wave, that neither theory alone conveys its complex reality, and that no broader framework allows us to grasp it more clearly are today everyman's truths. But that a similar approach is demanded for most social science concepts is still news for many.

Ivan Illich
GENDER

EXERCISES

1. Define male/female, masculine/feminine. List the attributes of each (strong, weak, etc.) List any exceptions that you can think of.

2. List the attributes of masculine and feminine as you believe someone of the opposite sex would.

3. Take any piece of writing, a newspaper article, a short story by you or someone else, and change the sex of the main character. Describe how the story and the other characters are affected.

4. Define masculine and feminine as you think your parents would. Compare its details to your list of attributes.

5. Define masculine and feminine as someone from another culture might. Someone from China, for example.

6. Imagine a world in which there is no male and no female. Write a short story which takes place in that world.

7. What is gender? Does it refer to biological sex differences or is it psychological and cultural, subject to variations both by individual preference and by social definition? If the latter is true, do you believe there are any differences between men and women aside from the obvious biological ones?

8. Describe a "super-masculine" man and a "super-feminine" woman. Put them in dialogue with each other.

9. Describe your own personality in terms of which traits you think of as masculine or feminine. Try to trace the origins or development of these traits in your own family experience.

10. List attributes of a human being that have nothing to do with gender.

11. Give a short history of your life as if you had been born the opposite sex.

12. Are the sexes really opposite? Write for 20 minutes.

LANGUAGE

Language uses us as much as we use language. As much as our choice of forms of expression is guided by the thoughts we want to express, to the same extent the way we feel about the things in the real world governs the way we express ourselves about these things. . . .

If a little girl "talks rough" like a boy, she will normally be ostracized, scolded, or made fun of. In this way society, in the form of a child's parents and friends, keeps her in line, in her place. This socializing process is, in most of its aspects, harmless and often necessary, but in this particular instance—the teaching of special linguistic uses to little girls—it raises serious problems, though the teachers may well be unaware of this. If the little girl learns her lesson well, she is not rewarded with unquestioned acceptance on the part of society; rather, the acquisition of this special style of speech will later be an excuse others use to keep her in a demeaning position, to refuse to take her seriously as a human being. Because of the way she speaks, the little girl—now grown to womanhood—will be accused of being unable to speak precisely or to express herself forcefully. . . .

It will be found that the overall effect of "women's language"—meaning both language restricted in use to women and language descriptive of women alone—is this: it submerges a woman's personal identity, by denying her the means of expressing herself strongly, on the one hand, and encouraging expressions that suggest triviality in subject matter and uncertainly about it; and, when a woman is being discussed, by treating her as an object—sexual or otherwise—but never a serious person with individual views. Of course, other forms of behavior in this society have the same purpose; but the phenomena seems especially clear linguistically.

The ultimate effect of these discrepancies is that women are systematically denied access to power, on the grounds that they are not capable of holding it as demonstrated by their linguistic behavior; and the irony here is that women are made to feel that they deserve such treatment, because of inadequacies in their own intelligence and/or education. But in fact it is precisely because women have learned their lessons so well that they later suffer such discrimination.

Robin Lakoff
LANGUAGE AND WOMAN'S PLACE

EXERCISES

1. Create a dialogue which illustrates the use of "woman's language." Be conscious of the ways in which such language limits access to power.

2. Answer the question: Do you believe there is a "women's language"?

DEFENSIVE FEMINISM

Feminism literally began on the defensive, i.e., as a reaction to anti-female or conservative sentiments, forces or policies which did not allow a woman the same individual, social or political rights as a man. For instance, Mary Woolstonecraft's VINDICATION OF THE RIGHTS OF WOMEN was inspired when Tallyrand decreed that the government educate children for free: but only the boys. Earlier, the misogynist work *Roman de la Rose* led Christine de Pisan (1364-1430) to write a defense of women which pointed out that all women weren't bad, only some of them. When she was viciously attacked for daring to speak up at all, she wrote a rebuttal in which she claimed that women were *superior* to men.

Kimberley Snow
PhD Dissertation, University of Kentucky, 1979

EXERCISES

1. Use the above facts to explain why a certain strident note keeps creeping into feminist arguments.

2. Try to formulate a feminist argument that isn't polarized, defensive, or dualistic.

In Chinese philosophy, Yin (woman) and Yang (man) are terms used for complementary opposites—earth and heaven, darkness and light, weakness and strength, female and male—which find balance in the Tao or the "Way."

TRANSCENDING DUALISM WHILE WHIPPING EGG WHITES INTO HIGH, STIFF PEAKS

When I worked my way through graduate school as a chef, as I prepared *Quenelles de Brochet* or *Spezzatino di Pollo,* I'd think about the dissertation that I didn't have time to write. My topic: "Feminism and Dualism," a subject with neither end nor mercy. The first part was easy, how feminist argument springs up when opposed ideas of masculine and feminine become polarized, how feminist thought and action struggle to rebalance these forces, to overcome stasis. But something about *dualism* kept eluding me, especially the ways in which dualism related to discrete concepts of masculine and feminine. Then, one afternoon while making a chocolate mousse, I understood what I'd been talking about.

I'd carefully separated the yolks from the whites, putting them each in their own identical grey bowls, fat yellow moons and a little glaucous sea. Gently sprinkled sugar over the thick, rich yellows, adding dark chocolate melted with butter. As I stirred, the egg mixture darkened, thickened. I whipped the whites in the other bowl until they stood frothy and unspotted, the purest white. In contrast, the container of dense chocolate seemed laden with the dark sexuality of some brooding seducer in a *fin de siecle* drawing.

Visually, at least, the contents of the two bowls loomed up as opposites, as yin and yang, one light, dry, the other dark, heavy, wet. But which should be called the male, which the female? I'd seen the white purity as virginal female, but in Taoism, the woman would be aligned with the wet darkness of yin. If we go from West to East, do we switch the alignments of masculine and feminine? And what of the values attributed to each side? Would the passivity and masochism the Freudians assigned to women in the West, be seen as Eastern virtues of equanimity and compassion? And then? What else would change? Everything?

As I moved ⌐n to the final step of combining the mousse, folding the heavy brown globs into the stark purity of the egg whites. . . the blending seemed almost a desecration. But as the commingled mixture took on its own creamy texture in a willing seduction, came an orgy of pleasures as the dark entered the whites and the envaginated light penetrated and enfolded and merged with the dark.

Soon I'd forgotten about opposites altogether, disappearing into the food. Mixing, remembering how men and women merge as seamlessly as yin and yang become the Tao. Mixing, understanding why the union of man and woman goes beyond thought of self and other.

Mixing, mingling. Skin on skin, fur on fur, tongue on nipple. Goatleg sliding goatleg. Down, backward, falling though the trapdoors of self, into the river of male and female together... loving, mating, bonding without thought of hesitation, no more able to keep separate boundaries than the egg whites and the chocolate coming together in shared wetness and fecundity could ever again live apart.

I understood then that it didn't matter which side is called masculine, which feminine, but as long as I viewed them as opposites, I'd continue to create—and strive to overcome—dualism after dualism. Only when I disappeared into the action, when I myself became the mixing, enfolding dark into white, did I free myself from a sense of separation, opposition, alienation.

Every time I try to theorize feminism and dualism, my thoughts harden and turn grey, like chocolate that's been left too long in the cold. But I understood it all that afternoon in the hot restaurant kitchen.

Kimberley Snow

EXERCISES

1. Describe your yang energy. Describe your yin energy. Make a list of your yang & yin qualities on same sheet of paper. Or they complementary? In opposition? Interactive?

2. Write a short story about yin and yang; how they meet, what happens to them over time.

An understanding of Carl Jung's terms "anima" and "animus" allows us to ask a whole different set of questions about gender. Perera's short and wise book suggests, among other things, that we women are just beginning to learn to deal with our "animus" power. Here she notes that women have yet to uncover true female power since we've been acting out a limited version of femininity which is usually defined in relationship to the masculine. The definitions are from Perera's glossary.

ANIMUS-EGO

Anima (Latin, "soul"). The unconscious, feminine side of a man's personality. She is personified in dreams by images of women ranging from prostitute and seductress to spiritual guide (Wisdom). She is the Eros principle, hence a man's anima development is reflected in how he relates to women. Identification with the anima can appear as moodiness, effeminacy, and oversensitivity.

Animus (Latin. "spirit"). The unconscious, masculine side of a woman's personality. He personifies the Logos principle. Identification with the animus can cause a woman to become rigid, opinionated, and argumentative. More positively, he is the inner man who acts as a bridge between the woman's ego and her own creative resources in the unconscious.

***

The problem is that we who are badly wounded in our relation to the feminine usually have a fairly successful persona, a good public image. We have grown up as docile, often intellectual, daughters of the patriarchy, with what I call "animus-egos." We strive to uphold the virtues and aesthetic ideals which the patriarchal superego has presented to us. But we are filled with self-loathing and a deep sense of personal ugliness and failure when we can neither meet nor mitigate the superego's standards of perfection.

One woman with more than a decade of Jungian analysis told me recently, "I have spent years trying to relativize something I never had—a real ego." And indeed she has only an animus-ego, not one of her own, with which to relate to the unconscious and the other world. Her identity is based on personal adaptations to what her animus tells her should be, so she adapts to and rebels against the projections hooked onto her; thus she has almost no sense of her own personal core identity, her feminine value and standpoint. For what has been valued in the West in women has too often been defined only in relation to the masculine: the good, nurturant mother and wife; the sweet, docile, agreeable daughter; the gently supportive or bright, achieving partner. As many feminist writers have stated through the ages, this collective model (and the behavior it leads to) is inadequate for life; we mutilate, depotentiate, silence, and enrage ourselves trying to compress our souls into it, just as surely as our grandmothers deformed their fully breathing bodies with corsets for the sake of an ideal.

> Sylvia Brinton Perera
> DESCENT TO THE GODDESS:
> A Way of Initiation for Women

EXERCISES

1. Describe your own animus-ego.

2. Define and describe your anima-ego.

3. How can female power find and express itself in a world (say the corporate) that is a full blown expression of the male power model?

SEARCH FOR THE GODDESS

When people talked about finding their goddess, I used to feel sorry for myself that I hadn't encountered Her in my own life. After discovering the book DESCENT TO THE GODDESS, which gives a Jungian reading of female power, I realized I had, indeed, descended to the goddess through my writing about Chef, a character in a play called DRAGON SOUP & OTHER SENSATIONS I had written years before. Chef arrived full blown, became the moral center of the drama at the same time she never gave an inch of body or sexual power away. Yet she wasn't connected with language at all, but was a sort of idiot savant.

In a visual sense, early on I visualized Chef as Gussie, the cook who worked for us when I was growing up. She wouldn't let me in her nice clean kitchen, for even then food flew through the air when I cooked. There is a scene in the play where Chef orders her helper out of her kitchen which is based directly on a childhood memory/experience. In writing about Chef (or standing slightly aside in awe as she took over my keyboard and wrote about herself), I always felt happy in her presence. She had the heavy sort of industrial strength power of a dynamo, released, unblocked.

Here is Chef.

ACT I, Scene 2

LUNCH IS OVER. THE WAITER'S STATION AND DINING ROOM HAVE BEEN REMOVED AND THE KITCHEN IS IN FULL VIEW. LIGHTING IS VERY DIM. KITCHEN HAS THE AIR OF AN ANIMAL'S DEN, BROWN AND FURRY, YELLOW AND DARK LIKE AN UNDERGROUND CAVERN WHERE PERHAPS PRIMITIVE RITUALS ARE ENACTED. A FEW CANDLES BURN HERE AND THERE. MUTTERING AND SOUNDS OF SLAPPING ARE HEARD. GRADUALLY IT BECOMES CLEAR THAT CHEF IS ALONE IN THE KITCHEN, STANDING AT THE PREP TABLE SLAPPING AND SPANKING THE BEEF TENDERLOIN—A STANDARD CULINARY PRACTICE TO GET JUICES FLOWING. CHEF, VERY DARK, IS A HUGE WOMAN, MORE OF A FORCE OF NATURE THAN A HUMAN BEING. INSTEAD OF A CHEF'S HAT, SHE WEARS AN ODD ASSORTMENT OF LEATHER STRAPS HUNG WITH VARIOUS INSTRUMENTS, SOME OF WHICH ARE NOT READILY IDENTIFIABLE. ODD THINGS HANG FROM HER HERE AND THERE. PERHAPS A STRING OF SAUSAGES OR A ROPE OF GARLIC COIL ABOUT HER NECK. ONE WOULDN'T BE SURPRISED TO SEE A LIVE SNAKE. DURING THE COURSE OF THE PLAY, SHE TAKES VARIOUS INSTRUMENTS FROM HER APRON AND USES

THEM TO WORK ON THE FOOD. THESE INTERACTIONS ABSORB
HER ATTENTION COMPLETELY. SHE GOES FROM DIRTY TO
FILTHY—SHE IS AS LIKELY TO OPEN THE REFRIGERATOR AND
DIP HER HANDS INTO THE COLD BABA GHANOUSH AND SLAP HER
FACE AND NECK WITH IT—TO COOL OFF—AS SHE IS TO GO TO THE
WATER TAP. SHE SENSES NO BOUNDARIES BETWEEN CONTAINER
AND CONTAINED. A TRUE PRIMITIVE, SHE DOES NOT SEPARATE
THE WORLD FROM HER PROJECTIONS. SHE ALONE PERCEIVES
THE DRAGON.

CHEF: Hey, hey, you pretty hunk. That get you going? That turn you on? Huh
huh. (EROTIC BESTIAL NOISES) That makes your JUICES flow? Huh huh.
Just wait till we get to the mustard! Gonna smear you up good, gonna make you
tingle all over your long self. Gonna be GOOD. Huh. Huh. Whew. Ha. Better
get to work on the soup.
(PASSING BY SPICES SHE POINTS FINGER ACCUSINGLY) Don't you
talk back to me. Had enough of you I have. . . You Juniper Berries. Perk up
there, got things for you to do tonight. Big things. Now you, you pretty
mushrooms. You want to go out with Marjoram or Oregano? What you in the
mood for pretty thing? So white and round. Well, you sit by him awhile and see
what you think. And you 'Prika, you stay out of this, what you know.

CHEF TAKES DOWN GIANT SOUP POT. MAKES PASSES OVER IT OF
A VAGUELY MAGICAL NATURE. SHE TURNS ON CASSETTE RE-
CORDER (AFRICAN DRUMS OR PERHAPS RAVEL'S BOLERO) FROM
TIME TO TIME SHE HITS POT WITH A WOODEN SPOON OR BREAKS
INTO A DANCE, BOUNCING HEAVILY AS IF WAIST DEEP IN THICK
SOUP.

CHEF: DUM DE DE DUM DE DE. (DANCES) DUM DE DE DUM DE DE
SOUP soup gonna make some soup. Dum de de DUM de de. Soup, gonna make
some soup. Soup, gonna make some soup. (CALLS) Dragon. Hey Dragon.
Dragoooooonnnnnn. (CROSSES TO BROOM CLOSET, THROWS OPEN
DOOR. DRAGON SITTING ON STOOL WRITING, HE PAYS NO ATTEN-
TION TO HER) Dragon. (WAITS) HEY, DRAGON.
DRAGON: (STILL WRITING) Um?
CHEF: Dragon. Needs your help. You busy?
DRAGON: (COMING OUT OF CLOSET) Just working on a poem. What's
up?
CHEF: Need to get the Chef's Special.
DRAGON: Ah, the Chef's Special. (SNIFFING, CHEF BEGINS TO SNIFF

TOO) What sort of day is it?

CHEF: (SNIFFING) Well, sort of. . . kinda. . . (SNIFFS) Know what I mean?

DRAGON: (SNIFFS) A spicy sort of day.

CHEF: Yeah, ginger spicy.

DRAGON: Many surprises.

CHEF: Oh, boy. Loves surprises.

DRAGON: Hmm.

CHEF: What's you mean 'Hmm.'

DRAGON: Just Hmm. Great spectrum of surprises.

CHEF: (TO HERSELF) Spec Trum.

DRAGON: Reminds me a little of the day I came through. (SNIFFS DEEPLY) Yes, indeed. (BEAT) The day I came through and couldn't get back.

CHEF: (WHO LOVES TO HEAR THE DRAGON TALK) That the day of the big earthquake?

DRAGON: The very same. I'd only come in for dinner that night.

CHEF: How's the food?

DRAGON: Oh! Even then it was worth traveling for.

CHEF: Yeah? What'd you have?

DRAGON: We started with Winter Melon Soup.

CHEF: We?

DRAGON: My Dragon and I.

CHEF: Yeah?

DRAGON: Yeah. Then BANG. Everything changed.

CHEF: BANG! Loves to happen.

DRAGON: Winter Melon Soup all over everywhere, plaster falling, then the fire. . . smoke and confusion.

CHEF: Yeah? And.

DRAGON: When it was all over, I was alone and the coordinate point sealed off—no more traveling between dimensions. Can't get back at all. (SHAKES HEAD) Now there's a broom closet where the entry point used to be. Don't know if she made it or not.

CHEF: Your dragon?

DRAGON: For years I thought maybe she just went into shock, forgot who she was. Dragons do that. But I always thought that one day she'd come to herself, then find me here.

CHEF: Don't you still believe that?

DRAGON: That she'd forget who she was, for over 50 years?

CHEF: Well, sometimes stuff is hard to remember. . .

DRAGON: I believe she got back. I do. Probably assumed I was right behind her. And now she can't get back through.

CHEF: Sort of on the other side of the door scratching to get in?

DRAGON: (GIVING CHEF SIDEWAYS LOOK) I wouldn't have put it exactly like that.

CHEF: What if she's 'round and you don't recognize her?

DRAGON: It's true Dragons are masters of disguise. (BEAT) But we're also masters at uncovering disguises. No. She couldn't fool me. (FONDLY) Not for long.

CHEF: Ain't you used to it here yet?

DRAGON: They can't see me, that's the trouble.

CHEF: Hmphh. They can't see nothing.

DRAGON: Lost in the dream. If only they'd spend more time on what's important.

CHEF: Yeah, like food.

DRAGON: Exactly! They can only evolve through their senses. . .

In the end of DRAGON SOUP & OTHER INTENSE SENSATIONS, the Chef is revealed to be the missing dragon, and the two disappear together through the coordinate point.

In thinking about Chef as the Goddess, I came to realize that DRAGON SOUP was also a Jungian fable: The Dragon represented the collective unconscious, the source of creativity that springs not just through personal talents, but through cultural forms such as cuisine. In Jungian terms, the Dragon is the animus, the male/left brain counterpart of the right brain/female/ anima Chef. The Dragon operates in language, in poetry, which leads him into the holistic world the Chef operates in all the time. In the play, the anima is cut off from the animus since he can't recognize her in her "disguise." The Dragon—blinded by ego (in the sense of seeing himself as separate, not as egotistical)—can neither penetrate her disguise nor be perceived by the world from which he is separated. In the end, this separation is overcome and integration found. So I'd really written an optimistic fable of male and female together in the modern world.

Kimberley Snow

EXERCISES

1. Search—in your writings or life—for your encounter with the feminine, with the goddess. Write about her.

2. Look through your writings for a fable. Expand on it.

3. Read Jung. Experiment with archetypes.

4. Read Toni Woolf, Jung's guide & mistress, try to visualize and write out your own versions of the archetypes she adds to Jung's.

In 1963, Betty Friedan wrote THE FEMININE MYSTIQUE which is often credited with starting the modern feminism movement. In 1981, in THE SECOND STAGE, she pointed out that to be effective, the women's movement must continue to change and to grow. Here she sets out the guidelines for the next step.

THE SECOND STAGE

The second stage cannot be seen in terms of women alone, our separate personhood or equality with men.

The second stage involves coming to new terms with the family—new terms with love and with work.

The second stage may not even be a women's movement. Men may be at the cutting edge of the second stage.

The second stage has to transcend the battle for equal power in institutions. The second stage will restructure institutions and transform the nature of power itself.

The second stage may even now be evolving, out of or even aside from what we have thought of as our battle.

Betty Friedan
THE SECOND STAGE

EXERCISES

1. List what you think should be included in the second stage of feminism, and techniques that would be effective for achieving it. What do you, personally, plan to contribute?

2. Write an essay describing how close you think we are to the second stage in the United States.

On the first day in a women's studies class, I give out a questionnaire which includes the following question:

"ARE YOU A FEMINIST?"

RECENT STUDENT ANSWERS:

"No, I'm not a feminist because I think that feminism requires that one be highly self-conscious all the time. I'd have to be constantly looking at myself from the outside, trying to define my role as a woman and to fight for my rights as a woman. It seems to me that thinking this way all the time would narrow my outlook (I'd have to always be aware of what is or isn't chauvinistic) and I'd like to *try* to see things in more than that one light. For example, to a true feminist, both my relationship with the pervert on the bus last year and with Professor X would be very cut and dried (men feel threatened thus try to get power over women). And I don't want my thinking to be that cut and dried. And I'm self conscious enough as it is without being self- conscious as a woman, too."

***

"No, I'm not a feminist, but I believe in equal rights and equal pay for women."

***

"Well sure. I mean how can you NOT be a feminist if you are a woman. Growing up in the 70's I did not find the idea of reinventing women revolutionary. It was as familiar as the fact that men were capable of traveling to the moon, and as obvious. Women were visibly changing. Women workers smiling down from telephone poles and the seats of Mack trucks or becoming engineers and technicians all blurred together into a single idea, that a woman can do anything she wanted to."

EXERCISES

1. Are you a feminist? Expound on why or why not.

2. Visualize all the feminists you know. What traits do they have in common?

SEXISM

"A husband and a wife are one, and he is that one."

Folk saying, frequently quoted to explain a man's "natural" position as head of the household.

EXERCISES

1. Define sexism for yourself. For others.

2. Write down the most sexist remark you have ever heard. Describe the person who made it.

3. Write down the most sexist remark that you have ever made.

4. Distinguish between subtle and blatant sexism. Give examples.

5. Which of the following statements do you consider sexist?:
    (a) Women are generally more conscious than men.
    (b) Women are not as strong as men.
    (c) Women need to be protected.
    (d) Women are too emotional to be trusted in executive positions.

6. Make a list of ways to fight sexism.

7. Write a description of women from a male sexist point of view. Put yourself totally in his mind. Afterwards, analyze how you felt as you wrote.

8. Create a dialogue between a sexist male and a radical feminist.

9. Distinguish between paternalistic, sexist, macho, and very male.

10. Write a poem about the effects of sexism. Here's a sample:

TESTOSTERONE RISING

At first he showed some signs of the x-
chromosome they share, and so she
sailed out on his sentences
—tell it, tell it, brother-human!—
but soon enough the great wave climbs,
she's tossed about on surging foam,
testosterone rising, choppy seas
of testosterone, and far out she's
alone, a long sad way from home.

Barry Spacks
BRIEF SPARROW

WOMEN AS MIRRORS

... Women have served all these centuries as looking-glasses possessing the magic and delicious power of reflecting the figure of man at twice its natural size. Without that power probably the earth would still be swamp and jungle. The glories of all our wars would be unknown. We should still be scratching the outlines of deer on the remains of mutton bones and bartering flint for sheepskins or whatever simple ornament took our unsophisticated taste. Supermen and Fingers of Destiny would never have existed. The Czar and the Kaiser would never have worn their crowns or lost them. Whatever may be their use in civilised societies, mirrors are essential to all violent and heroic action. That is why Napoleon and Mussolini both insist so emphatically upon the inferiority of women, for if they were not inferior, they would cease to enlarge. That serves to explain in part the necessity that women so often are to men. And it serves to explain how restless they are under her criticism; how impossible it is for her to say to them this book is bad, this picture is feeble, or whatever it may be, without giving far more pain and rousing far more anger than a man would do who gave the same criticism. For if she begins to tell the truth, the figure in the looking-glass shrinks; his fitness for life is diminished. How is he to go about giving judgement, civilising natives, making laws, speechifying at banquets, unless he can see himself at breakfast and at dinner at least twice the size he really is?

Virginia Woolf
A ROOM OF ONE'S OWN

EXERCISES

1. Describe at least two times in your life when you have reflected man at twice his size. Include your motives and the results.

2. Do you think anyone has ever done something similar for you?

3. Visualize yourself as a mirror. Describe the experience.

A glimpse into the ways in which men are affected by the women's movement can be found in the following selection in which a male student writes on what it is like to take a gender studies class.

A MALE PERSPECTIVE ON FEMINISM

I cannot exactly recall what made me want to enroll in Gender Studies. I do remember that I had originally put the class down as an alternative on my schedule sheet. When I got my schedule confirmation later that summer, I was enrolled in Gender Studies. It fit nicely into my schedule, and not wanting to deal with the hassles of schedule adjustment, I decided to keep an open mind and try the class out.

I was not without my doubts, however, most of them fuelled by other guys that I knew who warned me about the hazards of being one of the very few males in a class dominated by "raging penis-envy feminist types." "You'll be a constant target of reverse chauvinism," they would say, going on to discuss their impressions of "lesbian feminist types." I shrugged off their advice and opinions, partly because I didn't really take these people seriously, and partly because I know some cool people who are part of the women's movement. Also, I knew at least one other guy who would be in the class with me. The only things that I remained really apprehensive about were the large reading list and the long paper assignments.

Once in the class I found little reason to drop it. I found the professor to be very charming and sharp-witted, and the other students were equally pleasant. Furthermore, the reading turned out to be a refreshing break from the old Renaissance and 18th century stuff I had been reading in other classes, and so it was easier to get into.

As far as the actual experience of being an average male in a women's studies course, I didn't at the time notice any significant feelings of awkwardness or enlightenment, but in retrospect, I feel that the class changed me to a certain extent. Not that I walked in an asshole and came out an angel, so to speak. I considered myself at the time to be a conscientious and open minded person. When class discussions about events on campus (such as rape) or about the novels pinpointed a particular type of male as a jerk, either for his thoughts or for his actions, I did not feel that I myself was being associated with that person, and so rather than feeling defensive during the discussion, I automatically sympathized with the female position and was in total agreement that the male character type being attacked in the class was a bad one. While reading the novels, I never once felt that the male characters were created as "straw men," make to look stupid or evil only to be knocked down by superior female wisdom.

The way that I feel changed now by the class is that I tend to be more tuned in to the injustices towards women than I had previously been. Like I said, it wasn't that I did not already agree with any of the positions taken by the women's movement or by feminist writers. However, being male and growing up in a male-dominated culture, one tends to take many things for granted that in many ways are injurious to the other sex, and I am now more alarmed by such things than before. When I read a novel now and the female character is relegated to a supporting or a helpless role, it strikes a chord in me that such things are unfair and shouldn't be, whereas before I may not have noticed such a thing. It's similar to the race situation. I don't consider myself a racist, but being white, it's hard to always think of things in terms of how they would be viewed through non-white eyes, and so many "little things" tend to be taken for granted.

Now I tend to see things more through both male and female perspectives. Not that I will ever totally see life through a woman's eyes, but I am now more aware of the situation of women than I was before. There are other factors beside taking this class that contributed to this. For one thing, I have been deeply involved with a feminist woman and this undoubtedly affected my thinking along these lines.

One thing for certain is that this class had a very significant effect on the way that I view literature. I learned to read with an added awareness of how a woman might feel about the work I am reading. I feel that I benefitted tremendously from reading women novelists and poets, as this had broadened my perspective on the body of literature as a whole. It is sad to think that one could graduate with a degree in English without having read a woman author.

Another thing that impressed me about the class was the paper assignment which was very challenging. I had never thought of how difficult it might be to envision life through a woman's eyes until I tried to write a story with a female protagonist. It enabled me to see how fake some female characters are in novels written by some men. Such men seem to stereotype their female characters, and this is more obvious to me now.

I was never made to feel stupid or uncomfortable in the class, but as the class progressed, I gradually learned to become aware of how women are made to feel in this male-oriented culture, and therefore I am much more tuned in to social injustices towards others in general and women in particular than I was before. My respect for those guys who warned me against my taking this course has vanished. However, in their case, I do not think that even this class would turn them around, because they are part of a stubbornly proud macho-male subculture that refuses to learn better. If these types come around at all, I am afraid that it would have to be on their own because right now their pride stands in the way and they would simply laugh away the voice of common sense and reason. Those guys out there who would benefit from Gender Studies most are perhaps guys like I was before taking this class, who think of themselves as conscientious, open minded and basically nice persons, but who do not *really* think on a daily basis, as they observe the world about them or read about it, of what it would be like to be in someone else's shoes.

Student,
University of California at Santa Barbara

EXERCISES

1. Pick a man you know well and describe the changes he has gone through in the past ten years.

2. Write a short play about a man who becomes liberated. Decide what the word "liberated" means to you—and to him.

3. If you are female, imagine yourself as a male and write three of the exercises in this book from that point of view.

In the one woman show, SEARCH FOR SIGNS OF INTELLIGENT
LIFE IN THE UNIVERSE, Lily Tomlin plays a number of different
characters, beginning with Trudy the Baglady.

TRUDY THE BAGLADY

Here we are, standing on the corner of
"Walk, Don't Walk."
You look away from me, tryin' not to catch my eye,
but you didn't turn fast enough, *did* you?
. . .

I know what you're thinkin'; you're thinkin' I'm crazy.
You think I give a hoot? You people
look at my shopping bags,
call me crazy 'cause I save this junk. What should we call the
ones who
buy it?

It's my belief we all, at one time or another
secretly ask ourselves the question,
"Am *I* crazy?"
In my case, the answer came back: A resounding
YES!
. . .

You think too long about infinity, you could go
stark raving mad.
But I don't ever want to sound negative about going crazy.
I don't want to overromanticize it either, but frankly,
goin' crazy was the *best* thing ever happened to me.
I don't say it's for everybody;
some people couldn't cope.

But for me it came at a time when nothing else seemed to be
working. I got the kind of madness Socrates talked about,
"A divine release of the soul from the yoke of
custom and convention." I refuse to be intimidated by
reality anymore.
After all, what is reality anyway? Nothin' but a
collective hunch. My space chums think reality was once a
primitive method of
crowd control that got out of hand.
In my view, it's absurdity dressed up

in a three-piece business suit.

I made some studies, and
reality is the leading cause of stress amongst those in
touch with it. I can take it in small doses, but as a lifestyle
I found it too confining.
It was just too needful;
expected me to be there for it *all* the time, and with all
I have to do—
I had to let something go.

Now, since I put reality on the back burner, my days are
jam-packed and fun-filled. Like some days I go hang out
around Seventh Avenue; I love to do this old joke:
I wait for some music-loving tourist from one of the hotels
on Central Park to go up and ask someone,
"How do I get to Carnegie Hall?"
Then I run up and yell,
"Practice!"
The expression on people's faces is priceless. I never
could've done stuff like that when I was in my *right* mind.
I'd be worried people would think I was *crazy*.
When I think of the fun I missed,
I try not to be bitter.

See, the human mind is kind of like. . .

a pinata. When it breaks open,
there's a lot of surprises inside. Once you get the pinata
perspective, you see that losing your mind
can be a peak experience.

> Jane Wagner
> SEARCH FOR SIGNS OF INTELLIGENT LIFE
> IN THE UNIVERSE

EXERCISES

1. Ask yourself the question: "Are you crazy?" Explain your answer.

2. Create a dialogue between yourself and Trudy's "friends from space."

3. Write a short essay on your views of "reality."

4. If you've ever cracked open the pinata of the mind, what were some of the surprises you found?

While some women in the movement have been fighting on the political front, others have concentrated on looking in the past for the roots of women's power.

WITCHCRAFT

From earliest times, women have been witches, *wicce*, "wise ones"—priestesses, diviners, midwives, poets, healers, and singers of songs of power. Woman-centered culture, based on the worship of the Great Goddess, underlies the beginnings of all civilization. . . . Her priestesses discovered and tested the healing herbs and learned the secrets of the human mind and body that allowed them to ease the pain of childbirth, to heal wounds and cure diseases, and to explore the realm of dreams and the unconscious. Their knowledge of nature enabled them to tame sheep and cattle, to breed wheat and corn from grasses and weeks, to forge ceramics from mud and metal from rock, and to track the movements of moon, stars, and sun.

Witchcraft, "the craft of the wise," is the last remnant in the west of the time of women's strength and power. Through the dark ages of persecution, the covens of Europe preserved what is left of the mythology, rituals, and knowledge of the ancient matricentric (mother-centered) times. . . .

When Christianity first began to spread, the country people held to the old ways, and for hundreds of years the two faiths coexisted quite peacefully....

But in the thirteenth and fourteenth centuries, the church began persecution of witches, as well as Jews and "heretical" thinkers. Pope Innocent the VIII, with his Bull of 1484, intensified a campaign of torture and death that would take the lives of an estimated 9 million people, perhaps 80 percent of whom were women.

The vast majority of victims were not coven members or even necessarily witches. They were old widows whose property was coveted by someone else, young children with "witch blood," midwives who furnished the major competition to the male-dominated medical profession, free-thinkers who asked the wrong questions.

Memory of the true craft faded everywhere except within the hidden covens. With it, went the memory of women's heritage and history, of our ancient roles as leaders, teachers, healers, seers. Lost, also, was the conception of the Great Spirit, as manifest in nature, in life, in woman. Mother Goddess slept, leaving the world to the less than gentle rule of God-Father.

The Goddess has at last stirred from sleep, and women are reawakening to our ancient power. The feminist movement, which began as a political, economic, and social struggle, is opening to a spiritual dimension. In the process, many women are discovering the old religion, reclaiming the word *witch* and, with it, some of our lost culture.

Witchcraft, today, is a kaleidoscope of diverse traditions, rituals, theologies, and structures. But underneath the varying forms is a basic orientation common to all the craft. The outer forms of religion—the particular words said, the signs made, the names used—are less important to us than the inner forms, which cannot be defined or described but must be felt and intuited.

The craft is earth religion, and our basic orientation is to the earth, to life, to nature. There is no dichotomy between spirit and flesh, no split between Godhead and the world. The Goddess is manifest in the world; she brings life into being, *is* nature, *is* flesh. Union is not sought outside the world in some heavenly sphere or through dissolution of the self into the void beyond the senses. Spiritual union is found in life, within nature, passion, sensuality—through being fully human, fully one's self.

Our great symbol for the Goddess is the moon, whose three aspects reflect the three stages in women's lives and whose cycles of waxing and waning coincide with women's menstrual cycles. As the new moon or crescent, she is the Maiden, the Virgin—not chaste, but belonging to herself alone, not bound to any man. She is the wild child, lady of the woods, the huntress, free and untamed—Artemis, Kore, Aradia, Nimue. White is her color. As the full moon, she is the mature woman, the sexual being, the mother and nurturer, giver of life, fertility, grain, offspring, potency, joy—Tana, Demeter, Diana, Ceres, Mari. Her colors are the red of blood and the green of growth. As waning or dark moon, she is the old woman, past menopause, the hag or crone that is ripe with wisdom, patroness of secrets, prophecy, divination, inspiration, power—Hecate, Ceridwen, Kali, Anna. Her color is the black of night.

The Goddess is also earth—Mother Earth who sustains all growing things, who is the body, our bones and cells. She is air—the winds that move in the trees and over the waves, breath. She is the fire of the hearth, of the blazing bonfire and the fuming volcano; the power of transformation and change. And she is water—the sea, original source of life; the rivers, streams, lakes and wells; the blood that flows in the rivers of our veins. She is mare, cow, cat, owl, crane,

O

flower, tree, apple, seed, lion, sow, stone, woman. She is found in the world around us, in the cycles and seasons of nature, and in mind, body, spirit, and emotions within each of us. Thou are Goddess. I am Goddess. All that lives (and all that is, lives), all that serves life, is Goddess.

Because witches are oriented to earth and to life, we value spiritual qualities that I feel are especially important to women, who have for so long been conditioned to be passive, submissive and weak. The craft values independence, personal strength, *self*—not petty selfishness but that deep core of strength within that makes us each a unique child of the Goddess.

Starhawk
WOMANSPIRIT RISING
ed. Carol P. Christ and Judith Plaskow

EXERCISES

1. Write a short story about a witch (a) in prehistoric times (b) in the 15th century (c) today.

2. Write for 20 minutes on how you feel about using the terms witchcraft and/or goddess. What—if any—are the drawbacks of using this vocabulary today? Can we as women incorporate mythic and archetypal powers without using such terms? How?

3. Visualize a witch. Visualize a goddess. Visualize The Feminine. Compare and contrast.

In a land called Ata, the dream is more important than the waking life. Here, a native of Ata is trying to explain this country to a man who has recently intruded from Earth, explaining that from time to time someone from Ata goes back to Earth to try to save it. The man objects to what he perceives as a needless "sacrifice."

DREAMS

"How can death be a sacrifice? Death is only release into dreams; it can only be bad if one's dreams are bad. But to be sent into the world you left. . . can you imagine what that is like for a person used to the ways of Ata, used to living for his dreams? A world where all is donagdeo [against the way], where the most admired are the furthest from their dreams. Where empty speech is praised. Where noise is constant. Where people learn hate and suspicion of all, even of those they sleep with. Where people must feed themselves, or have the food snatched away from them. Where instead of the sacred dreams of the la-ka [big tent] people fill themselves with diversions that are like painkillers, only adding addiction to dis-ease. There all the people are like starving beasts, catching a glimpse from time to time of the great feast that lies before them, but kept from it by an invisible wall of fear and pride and superstition, crying, clawing at one another, despairing, and, by their acts, creating nightmares so that they learn to despise and fear that which would save them. . ."

"Then why send someone back?"

"All that I have described. Is it true of the world you left?"

"Yes, it is true."

"And have you ever asked yourself, how is it that this world has not yet destroyed itself?"

"Yes, everyone asks that, especially these days."

"It would have destroyed itself. The complete disconnection from the dream, total donagdeo, is destruction. When that possibility is imminent, someone is called, some kin of Ata, someone very strong. This kin is sent back, is sacrificed, is sent to live among those on the edge of destruction. The human race is like a suicide, perched on the edge of a cliff, wavering, teetering. When she is about to fall over the edge, one of us goes out and, using all the strength he has, makes a wind that blows against the falling, keeps humanity wavering on the brink. Do you understand what I am telling you?"

Dorothy Bryant
THE KIN OF ATA ARE WAITING FOR YOU

EXERCISES

1. Keep a dream journal. Write immediately upon awaking and in as much detail as possible. At first, this may prove difficult but it gets easier as you go along. Notice how and if your dream life changes once you start writing dreams down.

2. Look for and write about patterns in your dreaming: fear, escape, sex, etc. What does this teach you about yourself?

3. Get in a dialogue with a character from a dream. Let it go where it wants to.

4. Turn a dream into a short story.

5. If you have serial dreams in which you return to the same dreamscape and have a different adventure, describe that dreamscape and the atmosphere surrounding that series of dreams. Recreate it as fully as possible.

6. List information you have received through dreams.

7. Create a dream for someone else in which you appear.

8. Go through your dream journal and pick one person who appears in your dreams most often. Write about that person, as he/she appears in your dream and in your waking life.

9. Ask others in your household about their dreams. Compare with yours.

10. Create a dream-poem.

M.F.K. Fisher is best known for her delightful writings about food, but here she takes up a different subject.

AGING

... So far, myself, I think I am in luck, because I was a lively, healthy child who wanted and got a great share of affection. I notice that as I get rid of the protective covering of the middle years, I am more openly amused and incautious and less careful socially, and that all this makes for increasingly pleasant contacts with the world. (It also compensates for some of the plain annoyances of decrepitude, the gradual slowing down of physical things like muscles, eyes, bowels. In other words, old age is more bearable if it can be helped by an early acceptance of being loved and of loving.)

The physical hindrances are of course important, no matter how little an old person manages to admit their dominance. As I write this I am well into my seventies, and I think that I have aged faster than meant to, whatever that means! (It means, for one thing, that I resent being stiff and full of creaks and twinges.) I did not plan to be the way I am, although I probably knew more than most of my peers about the inevitabilities of disintegration. Fortunately, though, because I met Sister Age so long ago, I can watch my own aging with a detachment she has taught me. I know about the dismays and delights of my condition, and wish that all of us could prepare ourselves for them as instinctively and with as much outside help as we do those of puberty, adolescence, pregnancy, menopausal and climacteric changes. . . .

The Aging Process is a part of most of our lives, and it remains one we try to ignore until it seems to pounce upon us. We evade all its signals. We stay blandly unprepared for some of its obnoxious effects, even though we have coped with the cracked voices and puzzling glands of our emerging natures, and have been guided no matter how clumsily through budding love-pains, morning-sickness, and hot flashes. We do what our mentors teach us to do, but few of us acknowledge that the last years of lives, if we can survive to live them out, are as physically predictable as infancy's or those of our full flowering. This seems impossible, but it is true.

M.F.K. Fisher
SISTER AGE

EXERCISES

1. Write a story set in an old people's home.

2. Write a monologue from an aged person's point of view. If you are young, you might want to "become" one of your grandparents, then try to experience the process through them.

GRIEF

When someone you love dies, you have a feeling of numbness; a yearning; and a protest. You have lost part of yourself; you feel disorganized; and you do much crying. You're restless, and you may feel guilty. Perhaps you could have helped the one who died but you do not know how. You are angry because the person died, and you are angry at the world. You feel so alone, and loneliness is one of the biggest problems of grief. It is your problem and you have to solve it alone.

Elizabeth Kubler-Ross
DEATH: THE FINAL STAGES OF GROWTH

EXERCISES

1. Write about the death of a loved one.

2. Write about loss: start before you experienced the loss, appreciate what you had, then write about how the loss occurred, and what changes the absence has created in your life.

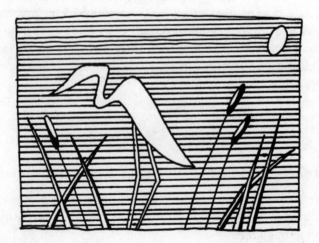

Laura Huxley has created a number of different exercises geared towards growth, integration, and increased consciousness. Below is one of the more dramatic.

ATTEND YOUR FUNERAL

Be sure that you will be alone for about two hours. Make certain there will be no telephone calls, bells, or other interruptions.

Have the room comfortably dark or dimly lighted.

Lie down on your bed or sofa or on the floor.

Let your body go. Imagine that the life is out of it. Do not speak or move.

Imagine that you have died. Your body is passive, lifeless, useless. Your body is discarded. Your funeral is about to take place.

You are now going to your own funeral.

Look at the people who have come to your funeral. What do they feel? How do they look at your body? Do they need consolation? Are they happy to be alive? Would *they* like to be dead? What are their emotions?

Look at the people coming to say a last goodby to this discarded body. Look at each of them. Is there one among them to whom you would like to say something, to explain something, to express a certain feeling? You cannot do it. Without your power of speech, of writing, of moving—without your body you can do nothing.

Look again at the people who attend your funeral. What would you like to say to each of them, if you could speak? How would you express yourself to this or that person, if you had a body? If looking at someone at your funeral makes you want to cry—then do cry, deeply and freely. You have every right to your tears.

Do you have a problem which has been difficult to solve? Do you have a decision which had been difficult to make? Your problem, your decision, will most probably be clarified at this moment.

Did you look at the flowers people sent you? What kind are they? How many are there? Did the people try to suit the preferences of the person you were? Or did they only do what they thought they ought to do?

Is anyone giving the eulogy? What is he saying? Does it seem to you sensible, reasonably true to you and your life?

Is there music? Has someone chosen it who knew what you liked, what you would prefer?

Now turn your attention to the person whom you disliked or hated or who irritated or repelled you more than any other in your life. Is there anything you want to say to that person?

Say it.

And now look at the one or ones you love most, at the one or ones to whom you are most grateful. Say whatever you wish or feel like saying. If tears do not let you speak, continue to cry and try to say what you feel.

This is your last party. Speak to everyone there, tell them all about yourself, about your mistakes and your suffering, about your love and your longings. No longer do you need to protect yourself, no longer do you need to hide behind a wall or a suit of armor. It is your last party: you can explode, you can be miserable or pitiful, insignificant or despicable. At your funeral you can be yourself.

And now it is over. Come back to your living body.

Acknowledge and respect it. Feel the life flowing in it. . .

Laura Huxley
YOU ARE NOT THE TARGET

EXERCISES

1. Try Huxley's exercise and then write about the experience of attending your own funeral.

2. Make a list of the things that you wanted to say to people at your funeral. Then decide whether or not you wish to tell them.

Visualization—creating a mental image on which to concentrate—is an important meditation technique in Tibetan Buddhism.

VISUALIZE PEACE

* Visualize an enemy, a neutral party, and a friend. Examine your attitude towards each, asking how extensive or permanent an enemy's harm or a friend's help might be. Note that friends and enemies are capable of change (even of turning into one another). If we can't clear the world of sharp objects, we can put on a pair of shoes.

* Recall kindness and help you have received. Remembered kindness creates a natural desire to repay in kind. Extend this feeling into the world.

* Consider how dependant we are on one another, even for the smallest items of convenience or survival. Imagine that everyone, enemies included, may have been in a past life—or might be in the future—one's mother.

* Imagine yourself as someone who neglects you. This should be a stimulant, out of self-interest, to remember the Golden Rule.

* Draw suffering into yourself; send happiness out towards others. Share both joy and pain.

> His Holiness the XIV Dalai Lama of Tibet
> Public speech, Santa Barbara

EXERCISES

1. Write for 20 minutes using one of the above techniques.

2. Try at least one other—perhaps the one that seems the strangest to you.

SHUG AND MISS CELIE TALK ABOUT GOD

Dear Nettie,

I don't write to God no more, I write to you.

What happen to God? ast Shug.

Who that? I say.

She look at me serious.

Big a devil as you is, I say, you not worried bout no God, surely.

She say, Wait a minute. Hold on just a minute here. Just because I don't harass it like some peoples us know don't mean I ain't got religion.

What God do for me? I ast.

She say, Celie! Like she shock. He gave you life, good health, and a good woman that love you to death.

Yeah, I say, and he give me a lynched daddy, a crazy mama, a lowdown dog of a step pa and a sister I probably won't ever see again. Anyhow, I say, the God I been praying and writing to is a man. And act just like all the other mens I know. Trifling, forgitful and lowdown.

She say, Miss Celie, You better hush. God might hear you.

Let 'im hear me, I say. If he ever listened to poor colored women the world would be a different place, I can tell you.

She talk and she talk, trying to budge me way from blasphemy. But I blaspheme much as I want to.

All my life I never care what people thought bout nothing I did, I say. But deep in my heart I care about God. What he going to think. And come to find out, he don't think. Just sit up there glorying in being deef, I reckon. But it ain't easy, trying to do without God. Even if you know he ain't there, trying to do without him is a strain.

I is a sinner, say Shug. Cause I was born. I don't deny it. But once you find out what's out there waiting for us, what else can you be?

Sinners have more good times, I say.

You know why? she ast.

Cause you ain't all the time worrying bout God, I say.

Naw, that ain't it, she say. Us worry bout God a lot. But once us feel loved by God, us do the best us can to please him with what us like.

You telling me God love you, and you ain't never done nothing for him? I mean, not go to church, sing in the choir, feed the preacher and all like that?

But if God love me, Celie, I don't have to do all that. Unless I want to. There's a lot of others things I can do that I speck God likes.

Like what? I ast.

Oh, she say. I can lay back and just admire stuff. Be happy. Have a good time.

Well, this sounds like blasphemy sure nuff.

She say, Celie, tell the truth, have you ever found God in church? I never did. I just found a bunch of folks hoping for him to show. Any God I ever felt in church I brought in with me. And I think all the other folks did too. They come to church to *share* God.

Some folks didn't have him to share, I said. They the ones didn't speak to me while I was there struggling with my big belly and Mr._children.

Right, she say.

Then she say: Tell me what your God look like, Celie.

Aw, naw, I say. I'm too shame. Nobody ever ast me this before, so I'm sort of took by surprise. Besides, when I think about it, it don't seem quite right. But it all I got. I decide to stick up for him, just to see what Shug say.

Okay, I say. He big and old and tall and graybearded and white. He wear white robes and go barefooted.

Blue eyes? she ast.

Sort of bluish-gray. Cool. Big though. White lashes, I say.

She laugh.

Why you laugh? I ast. I don't think it so funny. What you expect him to look like, Mr._?

That wouldn't be no improvement, she say. Then she tell me this old white man is the same God she used to see when she prayed. If you wait to find God in church, Celie, she say, that's who is bound to show up, cause that's where he live.

How come? I ast.

Cause that's the one that's in the white folks' white bible.

Shug! I say. God wrote the bible, white folks had nothing to do with it.

How come he look just like them, then? she say. Only bigger? And a heap more hair. How come the bible just like everything else they make, all about them doing one thing and another, and all the colored folks doing is gitting cursed?

I never thought bout that.

Nettie say somewhere in the bible it say Jesus' hair was like lamb's wool, I say.

Well, say Shug, if he came to any of these church we talking bout he'd have to have it conked before anybody paid him any attention. The last thing niggers want to think about they God is that his hair kinky.

That's the truth, I say.

Ain't no way to read the bible and not think God white, she say. Then she sigh. When I found out I thought God was white, and a man, I lost interest. You mad cause he don't seem to listen to your prayers. Humph! Do the mayor listen to anything colored say? Ask Sofia, she say.

But I don't have to ast Sofia, I know white people never listen to colored, period. If they do, they only listen long enough to be able to tell you what to do.

Here's the thing, say Shug. The thing I believe. God is inside you and everybody else. You come into the world with God. But only them that search for it inside find it. And sometimes it just manifest itself even if you not looking, or don't know what you looking for. Trouble do it for most folks, I think. Sorrow, lord. Feeling like shit.

It? I ast.

Yeah, It. God ain't a he or a she, but a It.

But what do it look like? I ast.

Don't look like nothing, she say. It ain't a picture show. It ain't something you can look at apart from anything else, including yourself. I believe God is everything, say Shug. Everything that is or ever was or ever will be. And when you can feel that, and be happy to feel that, you've found It.

Shug is a beautiful something, let me tell you. She frown a little, look out cross the yard, lean back in her chair, look like a big rose.

She say, My first step from the old white man was trees. Then air. Then birds. Then other people. But one day when I was sitting quiet and feeling like a motherless child, which I was, it come to me that feeling of being part of everything, not separate at all. I knew that if I cut a tree, my arm would bleed. And I laughed and I cried and I run all around the house. I knew just what it was. In fact, when it happen, you can't miss it. It sort of like you know what, she say, grinning and rubbing high up on my thigh.

Shug! I say.

Oh, she say. God love all them feelings. That's some of the best stuff God did. And when you know God loves 'em you enjoys 'em a lot more. You can just relax, go with everything that's going, and praise God by liking what you like.

God don't think it dirty? I ast.

Naw, she say. Not vain, just wanting to share a good thing. I think it pisses God off if you walk by the color purple in a field somewhere and don't notice.

What it do when it pissed off? I ast.

Oh, it make something else. People think pleasing God is all God care about. But any fool living can see it always trying to please us right back.

Yeah? I say.

Yeah, she say. It always making little surprises and springing them on us when us least expect.

You mean it want to be love, just like the bible say.

Yes, Celie, she say. Everything want to be loved. Us sing and dance, make faces and flower bouquets, trying to be loved. You ever notice that trees do everything to git attention we do, except walk?

Well, us talk and talk bout God, but I'm still adrift. Trying to chase that old white man out of my head. I been so busy thinking bout him I never truly notice nothing God make. Not a blade of corn (how it do that?) not the color purple (where it come from?) Not the little wildflowers. Nothing.

Now that my eyes opening, I feels like a fool. Next to any littlescrub of a bush in my yard, Mr._'s evil sort of shrink. But not altogether. Still, it is like Shug say. You have to git man off your eyeball, before you can see anything a'tall.

Man corrupt everything, say Shug. He on your box of grits, in your head, and all over the radio. He try to make you think he everywhere. Soon as you think he everywhere, you think he God. But he ain't. Whenever you trying to pray, and man plop himself on the other end of it, tell him to git lost, say Shug. Conjure up flowers, wind, water, and a big rock.

But this hard work, let me tell you. He been there so long, he don't want to budge. He threaten lightening, floods and earthquakes. Us fight. I hardly pray at all. Every time I conjure up a rock, I throw it.

Amen

Alice Walker
THE COLOR PURPLE

EXERCISES

1. Describe God.

2. Imagine different gods.

A dakini is a manifestation of female energy in Tibetan Buddhism, similar to the anima or feminine aspect in Jungian psychology. A dakini—literally "one who moves in the sky"—can be wrathful or peaceful, can appear as a goddess, a human being, or as an ever-changing flow of energy.

TWILIGHT LANGUAGE

In our culture, which is dominated by the rational, scientific point of view, we tend to think of language in a very limited way. But mystics and madmen have always maintained that there are other kinds of languages. These are languages which cannot be interpreted or understood by the rational left hemisphere of the brain. The Tibetan lamas speak of a language called "the secret signs and letters of the dakini" and another which is a secret code of Tantric terminology called "the twilight language."

The language of the dakini consists of letters and symbols which have no set translation. The ability to understand the meaning of this language is the province of only a very few—those who are in contact with the energy field of the dakini. It is a highly symbolic cipher which is so condensed that six or seven volumes of teachings could come out of a few letters.

. . . We can understand that the "twilight language" is an actual cipher which can only be understood by those blessed by the wisdom dakini. The way the language is translated is not with a dictionary and a grammar book, but through "another way of knowing" which comes from a space which is far from the sunlit rational world dominated by the logos, and at the same time it is not from the dark abyss of the unconscious but rather a twilight world where another function of the mind is possible. This is not merely the intuitive part of the mind, because even very sensitive people cannot understand the language of the dakini. It is a realm governed by the dakinis, and only those who can integrate into the symbolic world of the dakini can understand their half-concealed language.

. . . Twilight is the time between waking and sleeping, the conscious and the unconscious. It is a time when the switch over takes place, so there could be a gap, a crack in the wall of the ever-protective ego structure where significant communication from something beyond could take place.

Tsultrim Allione
WOMEN OF WISDOM

EXERCISES

1. At dusk, condense something you have written into the twilight language; hide it under a stone.

2. Visualize a dakini finding what you have written.

NAMING

Behind naming, beneath words, is something else. An existence named un-named, and unnameable. We give the grass a name, and earth a name. We say grass and earth are separate. We know this because we can pull grass free of the earth and see its separate roots—but when the grass is free, it dies. We say the inarticulate have no souls. We say the cow's eye has no existence outside ourselves, that the red wing of the blackbird has no thought, the roe of the salmon no feeling, because we cannot name these. Yet for our own lives we grieve all that cannot be spoken, that there is no name for, repeating for ourselves the names of things which surround what cannot be named. We say Heron and Loon, Coot and Killdeer, Snipe and Sandpiper, Gull and Hawk, Eagle and Osprey, Pigeon and Dove, Oriole, Meadowlark, Sparrow. We say Red Admiral and Painted Lady, Morning Cloak and Question Mark, Baltimore and Checkerspot, Buckeye, Monarch, Viceroy, Mayfly, Stonefly, Cicada, Leaf-hopper and Earwig, we say Sea Urchin and Sand Dollar, Starfish and Sandworm. We say mucous membrane, uterus, cervix, ligament, vagina and hymen, labia, orifice, artery, vessel, spine and heart. We say skin, blood, breast, nipple, taste, nostril, green, eye, hair, we say vulva, hood, clitoris, belly, foot knee, elbow, pit, nail, thumb, we say tongue, teeth, toe, ear, we say ear and voice and touch and taste and we say again love, breast and beautiful and vulva, saying clitoris, saying belly, saying toes and soft, saying ear, saying ear, ear and hood and hood and green and all that we say we are saying around that which cannot be said, cannot be spoken. But in a moment that which is behind naming makes itself known. Hand and breast know each one to the other. Wood in the table knows clay in the bowl. Air know grass knows water knows mud knows beetle knows frost knows sunlight knows the shape of the earth knows death knows not dying. And all this knowledge is in the souls of everything, behind naming, before speaking, beneath words.

Susan Griffin
WOMAN AND NATURE:
The Roaring Inside Her

EXERCISE

Do not write. Try to experience the space behind, between, and before words.

UTILIZING YOUR WRITING

"Writing is making sense of life."

Nadine Gordimer

USING JOURNALS FOR PERSONAL GROWTH

The exercises in this book may be used as a guide to help you get in touch with your most pressing personal issues. Transforming emotions and buried experiences into words is the first step towards getting them into consciousness where you can perhaps do something about them. Often you won't even know how you feel about something until you read what you have written.

After you've learned that writing can take you below a certain level of mind, then you're embarked on a very profound journey that is perhaps best not talked about too much. There is something out there/in here, something conscious that holds the world together, something that is knowable, something that can be known and understood in silence, in loneliness, something that reveals itself gradually or swiftly, something that can be taken away sometimes for weeks or even years. What to call it? To name it might destroy it, but let it work through you: trust it, trust yourself, trust the process that binds you both together. Trust and honor it. You have to be very quiet, very still to hear it, like catching a tune being played in the far distance. Learn to be still and to be quiet and let it work through you, heal you.

When writing primarily to chart your personal psychological process, you may want to adopt a few simple guidelines to act as touchstones. Rule One: Don't edit yourself as you go along. Let it all come out. Don't worry about final versions, editing, voice, sentence structure, stylistic devices, or any of that. This is for personal edification, not publication. Rule Two: Don't feel bad about what you've written. You've written it, not done it. Moreover, by writing it all, you're revealing emotions and thoughts that can help you figure out the big picture of your life.

EXERCISES

1. If you are in therapy, keep a separate notebook about what you are experiencing, processing, healing. At intervals in the process, try a few of the exercises entitled THE BIG PICTURE.

2. If you keep a journal, read through and figure out what your main psychological issues are. Then turn to the subject index of this book and do the applicable exercises.

TRANSFORMING JOURNAL MATERIAL INTO FICTION

Writing in a journal or keeping any kind of ongoing record of thoughts, activities, and events provides a storehouse of information when it comes to writing for publication. Letters and the writing exercises in this book can also be used to create fiction and poetry. But before you launch off, you must ask yourself if you really want to publish your work. Are you willing to make the enormous commitment of time and energy that a writing career demands? Do you want unknown eyes poring over your words? Would anyone else be interested in what you have to say? Not everything can or should be published. Perhaps your work is better written for yourself and shown to no one.

Or you may discover that you are comfortable publishing in certain literary forms, but not in others. Just recently I had a poem published. I hated the way it looked on the page, hated the exposure, the sense of having shared a private moment from ten years ago with uncaring strangers. I wanted to find and destroy every single copy of the magazine in which the poem appeared. As it happens, I don't feel that way about fiction or non-fiction, which is what I'll publish in the future, not poetry.

Despite such caveats, if something pushes you in the direction of "going public" over and over, then you probably do want to at least experiment in putting your journal work and exercises into fictional, perhaps publishable, form.

EXERCISES

1. Leaf through your journal and find a passage which seems very strong, very articulate. Copy it out and use it as the basis of a short story. Change the story as you go along, don't feel compelled to stick to "reality" either as you remember it or as it is recorded in your journal. Henry Miller once said, "I lie in order to be more true." Find a suitable passage in your journal and lie, lie, lie. Be true to the emotion of the situation, but be sure to disguise the event (especially if you are considering publication—thinly fictionalized stories have led to many lost relationships and even litigation).

2. If you keep letters (copies of yours or ones sent to you) look through them for a compelling incident. Use it for the basis of a poem or story.

3. Try the other exercises in this section.

THE BIG PICTURE

Sometimes it's helpful to think of your life in terms of major themes, issues, events and/or people. This is what I call the Big Picture. One easy way of seeing your personal Big Picture, the issues and feelings that comprise the colors in the mosaic of your life, is to use your journal or other writings. If you keep or have kept a journal, you can use the BIG PICTURE and the CLUSTERING THE BIG PICTURE exercises for personal growth and integration and/or to create the outline of a novel, short story, or play.

EXERCISES

1. Start a new section in your journal or a new notebook. Imagine your life as a book. Give it a title, divide it into sections, name the subdivisions. Write the index for the book of your life, labeling each chapter. Imagine marketing this book: where would it go in the bookstore: non-fiction, romantic novels, cookbooks, health section? Look around a bookstore with this in mind.

2. Return to your index of the book of your life. Close your eyes, point your finger to one of the chapter heads and start to write. Write for 20 minutes.

3. Close your eyes and page through your notebook. Elaborate on the last sentence on the page where you stop.

4. Reduce the events of any chapter to a telegram. This is an excellent exercise if you are wordy. In case you want to improve in this area, go through several of the readings in the book and condense them into a telegram.

5. SON OF BIG PICTURE: On a separate piece of paper, create a category called FAMILY. Go through the book of your life and record every name mentioned, skipping several lines for each entry. Now go back and free associate on each person, jotting down a telling word or two in the empty space between the names.

6. Return to SON OF BIG PICTURE. Close your eyes, put your finger on a name and write for 20 minutes without stopping. Keep doing this until you have written about each family name you recorded.

CLUSTERING THE BIG PICTURE

This is a project for a weekend when you have plenty of time. In order to do this series of exercises, you must first xerox everything in your notebook and journals, and have a pair of scissors handy. Sit in the middle of a rug or bed and sort your writing into piles around you as to recurrent subjects; for example, loneliness, parenting, love, career, school, etc. As you read through your journal, you will be able to decide what subjects to choose, but if you are uncertain about the method, consult CLUSTERING at the beginning of this book. Once you've sorted everything, look for particularly tall piles. Pick one up, read it through. Repeat until all piles are reviewed, thought about, sorted. Then go on to the exercises below.

EXERCISES

1. PEOPLE IN THE BIG PICTURE: Resort the piles in terms of the people in your life. Read each pile through, writing comments in the margins. Return to Relationship exercises for inspiration.

2. Pick one of the piles from the PEOPLE AND THE BIG PICTURE exercise, and write a chronological account of your relationship with that person. Write the same story, but from the other person's point of view. Wait a month, and retell the story from a third person's point of view. Do this for all the important people in your life.

3. OUTSIDE THE BIG PICTURE: Write three stories about yourself from the point of view of another person. Pick someone you know or make up a person. Use the results for the first chapter of a novel.

4. BIG PICTURE CROWD SCENE: Return to PEOPLE AND THE BIG PICTURE. Write a crowd scene of six of your people together: a family dinner, a reunion, a scene in a restaurant, whatever. Listen to what they are saying to each other. Turn the scene into a play.

5. MONEY AND THE BIG PICTURE: Return to your original piles and pick out all the references to money and/or work. Put them into some sort of order: try to let a structure emerge by using the clustering technique for sorting. If I were doing it, I would find that I had a whole, happy group talking about beautiful jackets I'd gotten on sale, while everything to do with job and making money in another pile seems to be written by someone male and older. When I think of the attitudes expressed in terms of gender,

I find that when it comes to spending money, I'm unreconstructed Southern female, while my ideas about making money are econo-feminist (I should support myself, women should get equal pay for equal work). I look further in my writings about making money and I find that I have a patriarchal streak; I don't just think in terms of family, but of empire.

6. MARKETPLACE: Return to MONEY AND THE BIG PICTURE. Extract all writings about your job or jobs. Put them in chronological order, tell your entire job history to a sympathetic friend. Give her (or him) a name, a face, healing powers.

7. GENDER AND THE BIG PICTURE: Return to your xeroxed journal. Sort through in terms of gender, as I did in MONEY AND THE BIG PICTURE. Write about what you find. For example, when I look through my own journals, I find that money isn't the only place where I hold contradictory attitudes that I associate with gender. In teaching, I also struggle to maintain a balance between two different models: one is warm, nurturing, accepting; the other distant, fact-oriented, and unforgiving.

8. BODY IN THE BIG PICTURE: Select passages from your journal writings that have to do with your bodily functions and body image. Read through and let a structure or a pattern emerge. Blank out your mind, then write for 20 minutes. This method may be repeated many times, used many different ways for all types of issues.

9. SPEECH AND THE BIG PICTURE: Re-sort your writings to find anything which has to do with speech, with communication, with language. Free write for 20 minutes on the way you have interfaced with the world though speech.

10. THE BIGGER PICTURE: Think about the world around you, the cosmos, the void, the ever-changing ground of the universe. Place your own BIG PICTURE in this context.

ON WRITING A NOVEL

Begin now. Novels take a long time.

The first thing to do is to go through all of your journals, calendars, records, notes to yourself, and exercises from BIG PICTURE. Cluster, mark, put in order.

Let the structure (which will later turn into the substructure) emerge. Customize your material: let it tell its own story. Even if you never want to write a novel, it is fun to see your life in terms of a book and to create yourself out of yourself, backwards, in high heels, dancing.

Try to dream your characters. Tell yourself that you will dream about them and it will increase your chances. Try to be them dreaming, write out their dreams.

Think of someone you know who has a distinctive way of speaking—an accent, a rhythm of speech, a certain speed. When you hear it, you know who is speaking. That's what 's called "voice" in writing. When you are telling a story in a novel, you need a voice. You also want to develop a different and distinct voice for each character. Try to hear your characters talk, write down what they are saying.

The quickest, easiest way I've found to develop characters through voice is to write a play. Or rather, write in play form: with minimum stage directions, all dialogue. In a play, everyone has to speak, has to show their motivation through speech. No falling back on summary or passive voice.

In the beginning of a novel, different voices often fight for dominance, for who is going to be in charge of telling the story. Let them all tell their stories separately. Xerox up these stories, cut them apart and use for scenes of dialogue in the novel.

Personally, as a writer, I prefer character to plot. I don't really care much about the plot line, to tell you the truth. I think of it as something I do for other people so they will know what is going on. But for me, I never think about plot until fairly late in the project. For me, character itself generates plot. One way to apply this is to take two or more characters from your writings, put them in a situation together, and listen to what they say to each other. Keep writing until a plot emerges. It is true that this story line is what keeps people reading, so once you've found a basic plot grounded in character, throw in a bit of extra tension to keep the reader going.

A first person point of view both limits and expands a novel. You can go deeper, more quickly (and use more from your journals) in first person than in a "social" point of view where you have to account for what each character knows and how she knows it. I find that it helps to write at least one draft in the first person, just to move the material from place to place. I can always go back and change "I" to "she."

When you feel written out on individual voices, stories, etc., xerox them all, sit in the middle of the bed or on the floor and spread the pieces around you. Use the clustering technique described in CLUSTERING THE BIG PICTURE on the pieces of the novel.

Work in scenes. Put together pieces that lean, for whatever reasons, towards one another. Work with the editing side of your brain, make decisions, cut, prune, slash, burn.

Paste up a new version; tie the parts together by short transitions between the pasted-in paragraphs of dialogue, description, etc. Just write down the first thing that comes to mind and keep moving. Xerox up a clean copy of this version and treat yourself to something wonderful for finishing the first draft of your novel.

This is one of my favorite stages in novel writing, when I can get continuous pagination for the first time, when a spine appears. Often whatever I've written has to be changed many times, but from this moment on I can look on my desk and *see* a book. And this calls for a celebration. Next, I usually let the manuscript sit for at least a month, sometimes for years. Then I return and repeat the cluster-xerox process all over again—several times. Nor do I know when a particular novel is going to reappear. I just wake up with it in my head. In the between times, it must be simmering down there in the great creative soup of the unconscious.

While I am in the middle of a writing project, I lead a parallel life. All the time I'm writing, I'm having multi-layered emotional responses to my past, persona, archetypes, fear, ego, plus the past, persona, etc. of all of my characters. When I'm writing hard, I live intensely, yet I am totally unaware of myself as a person, as an ego, as existing in time. If a relative stranger asked me what I'd been doing, I'd have to say, well, not much, sitting at the computer. But in sitting there, I've traveled from star to star, from psyche to psyche, wallowed in pain, found solace and clarification in play.

Once, using material from a therapist, I wrote a play about a multiple personality patient. The story was very painful; the woman herself had been severely abused and died very young. Still, I thought smugly to myself on my way to the computer, it's not *my* pain. But as I progressed in the writing, as I sat sobbing into the green words of light on the monitor in front of me, I realized that it had indeed become my pain. If I, the writer, didn't feel the emotion, how could I expect to move the audience? So, be careful what you put in your novel; the ideas and emotions pass through your psyche, creating patterns, whether you want them to or not.

When you're writing sensitive material or have "gone under" in a writing project, a great deal of emotion is displaced. I remember when with my husband—a fellow writer, plus first and finest editor—I had just taken my novel POWER TREE to the print shop to be copied on ivory classic laid 24 lb bond to go to my agent. We stopped by a restaurant filled with palm trees and mossy fountains to celebrate with brunch. The waiter brought us champagne, and after a half a glass, we both spontaneously burst into tears. All the emotional intensity we hadn't been able to feel for the past 24 hours of getting the final clean copy together and in order, suddenly popped forth like the cork from the bottle.

The waiter rushed over, concerned, leaning over us. "Are you all right?"

"Yes," we sobbed, "we're xeroxing."

"Writers," we heard him explain to another waiter as they moved a bushy palm tree in front of our table.

DEVELOPING A SHORT STORY

When staying with my sister once in South Carolina, I heard a story about Laura who had visited us that afternoon: Laura's mother had phoned one day to ask if she had anything to wear to her mother's funeral—she didn't want her daughter to show up in another tacky dress.

In the end, Laura's mother had come over, gone through Laura's closet, and couldn't find anything "suitable." The mother—rich, used to having her own way—took her daughter downtown to shop for a black silk dress which the daughter wasn't to wear to parties or dinners or anywhere at all: a dress meant only for her mother's funeral. The fact that Laura didn't own a good silk dress for herself—Laura had four children—and could have used one, didn't seem to cross the mother's mind. Every year, my sister told me, the mother—too cheap to buy her daughter a new dress—would haul Laura downtown to have the dress restyled.

Something about that story stayed in my imagination, grew there. For me, the story caught the power of a dominating Southern mother in a way that nothing else quite did. Then, years later, my sister told me the end of the tale, and I wrote the short story, "Funeral Dress." This is the sequence of composition the story went through, including its brief life as a one act play.

In the first version of the short story, I stayed close to Laura, who is married and has a large, happy family. Here's how I began:

FUNERAL DRESS: FIRST VERSION

"Maurina Elaine, do you have a dress for my funeral?"

7:30 a.m. phone call. Mother's Morning Call, Lane's husband had named it—always the signal that Rena Grace had been up all night working something out.

"Are you feeling unwell?" Lane asked her mother, not without a certain ironic overtone that went unnoticed.

***

The husband was dropped right away; the tension between the two women felt greater without a man in the picture. After many different drafts, I worked out a story in four scenes. Here are some samples of the project at this point:

Lane had been helping her mother sort through her closet when they came across a box marked FUNERAL in black magic marker. Lane started to open it when Rena Grace stopped her.

"Don't you bother with that. One of my children will take care of it."

"But, Mother," Lane looked at the old woman in alarm. "I *am* one of your children. I'm the only one left."

"Of course, I know that," Rena Grace huffed. "Of course I do."

A few days later, Lane received a 7:30am phone call from Rena Grace. Mother's Morning Call, a signal that Rena Grace had been working something out.

"Maurina Elaine, do you have a dress for my funeral?"

"I hadn't thought about it, Mother. Are you feeling unwell?"

"I'll have Harris run me by about two and we'll go to Bernaldo's and pick something out."

****

One by one the saleswomen in the small shop came up to say good afternoon to Miss Rena Grace, and to offer coffee and chocolate mint wafers. One of them, the youngest and newest on the staff of Bernaldo's, seemed to be resisting an impulse to curtsey.

Mrs. Carlson, the clerk who always waited on Rena Grace, and resembled her in body size and shape, held up four dark dresses. "Is this what you had in mind?"

"Not the wool. We want it for all seasons." Rena Grace surveyed the dresses critically. "Maybe the navy. Maybe the black with the shawl collar. Hm. I don't know about that other black. What do you think, Maurina Elaine?"

I think I'd like a scarf to go with my blue silk you hate so much. I could wear it to. . .

"Maurina Elaine?"

"I like the navy."

"Well, try it on. And the black with the shawl collar."

The dresses didn't fit. The navy almost did.

***

About a year later, Rena Grace made another morning call about the dress. "I think it will do again for this year."

"Yes, I think so. I haven't worn it."

"Well, that's good news. Estelle"—Rena Grace's cook of 25 years—"said she'd never seen you in it."

"It doesn't fit."

"It fits fine. Don't start that again."

"Anyway, I've got to get ready for work."

"Work? Oh, you mean the library."

"I *work* at the library."

"We had the dress altered. They sent me quite a bill."

"Breakfast. I have to go fix breakfast."

"Why are you working on Saturday?"

"We all have to work on Saturday now. I told you."

"That's right. I'm finding it harder and harder to remember things these days."

"Mother, I've told you at least five times that if you want to be counted as a full time staff member, you have to work on Saturday."

"Well, work part time. That's what you've been doing."

"I can't afford it since they raised my rent. I TOLD you that."

"As I say, I have a hard time remembering things."

***

The next year, Rena Grace was on her trip to Italy and sent a card telling Lane to get Bernaldo's to take up the hem of her funeral dress because skirts were very short in Europe. The year after that they added a black lace jabot, although Lane really wanted a white one. When wide shoulders came back in, they added thick pads which made Lane look so stylish Rena Grace seemed a little disappointed she didn't die while that fashion lasted.

***

"Well, did you ever!"

"Never."

Lane overheard them as she entered the crowded church and moved slowly down the aisle on the usher's arm.

"Rena Grace is going to jump right up out of her coffin." The old woman's whisper carried at least six pews.

Lane held a handkerchief to her mouth, pressing against a tide of unaccustomed emotion.

"Will you just look at that dress."

Surprised, Mrs. Carlson?

Lane passed her aunts, Maurina and Elaine, from whom she'd gotten her names, but not her skin. She pretended to sag a little so she could hear their muttered whispers.

"To think Maurina Elaine would dress like that at her own mother's funeral."

"Blood red."

"Maurina Elaine never did have a lick of sense about clothes. Rena Grace said it a hundred times."

Lane pressed the handkerchief harder to her mouth.

"And that hat!"

"Looks like she borrowed it from Estelle."

"That awful bunch of cherries!"

***

My editor had this to say about this early version: "I love your story until the end. Not that the end is, in itself, badly written but I think it's too pat. There's not enough story around it to make it work. I'm not sure what to suggest; I love all the scenes you have. Maybe an interwoven story about Lane, how she lives in between the sessions with her mother so that we feel her internal struggle. We see her always going along with Rena Grace and then bingo, the great rebellion when she dies. We need to know her better, feel for her more. This story cries out to be developed further."

I decided to develop the story into a play for a local one act contest. As I said in ON WRITING A NOVEL, there is no greater shortcut for me than to cast things into a play form. For one thing, I am forced to visualize the material and the setting in order to write out the stage directions; the characters speak their lines without the interruption of a narrator's (mine) voice, so I can just relax and let them say to each other whatever comes out. Also, in a play, the characters assume color, dimension, drama, that can then be put back into a short story or novel.

For example, Rena Grace's personality took on much more lifelike dimensions once I let her speak for herself. Here's a short excerpt from the play:

Rena Grace: I just don't want you to embarrass me with that blue silk you wore to Hattie's at Thanksgiving. I got to thinking last night and couldn't stop until I worked it out.

(PAUSE)

ELAINE: OK, worked WHAT out?

RG: Well, my funeral, of course. I planned the whole thing. (LIGHTS GO DOWN ON ELAINE AND UP ON CENTER STAGE) It will be at the First Presbyterian Church, of course. We'll bring dear Doctor Alexander out of retirement. I certainly don't want that young man they have now to do my service. Doesn't look more than 12 years old. (PAUSE) I don't care where he got his degree. I don't want him at MY funeral. I want it done right. All of it. No lilies. White carnations with a little touch of green asparagus fern. Closed casket. (MUSIC SWELLS) Bach. (LANE BEGINS TO WALK DOWN THE AISLE, SHE'S WEARING BLACK COAT, BLACK HAT WITH VEIL. SHE'S SOBBING LOUDLY, STYLIZED DISPLAY OF GRIEF.)

LANE: Mother, oh, Mother.

SPOT BACK TO RENA GRACE, FANTASY FADES...

I didn't win the local play contest, but I learned a great deal by dramatizing my material. First, I added a bit more background information so that the mother-daughter relationship made more sense. But more importantly, the characters became real to me. I felt much kinder towards Rena Grace, so when I wrote the final version of the story, I could be more than one-dimensional in portraying her. Also, I came to respect Lane, which I hadn't very much in the earlier versions. Now, I find myself wondering what happened to her after her mother's funeral, and plan to write more about her.

FUNERAL DRESS: PUBLISHED VERSION

The phone rang 14 times before Lane picked it up. 7:01 am. Mother's Morning Call.

"Maurina Elaine, do you have a dress for my funeral?"

"I hadn't thought about it, Mother. Are you feeling unwell?"

"I don't want you to embarrass me with that blue silk you wore to Hattie's at Thanksgiving."

"Could this wait until, say, after breakfast?"

"Aren't you up yet?"

Sigh.

"No, Maurina Elaine, I got to thinking last night and couldn't stop until I worked it out."

Pause. "Worked *what* out?"

"My funeral. I planned the whole thing. It'll be at First Presbyterian, of course, We'll have to bring dear Doctor Alexander out of retirement. I certainly don't want that young man they have now at *my* funeral. Doesn't look more than 12 years old. I don't care where he got his degree. I want it done right. All of it. White carnations with a little touch of green asparagus fern. Closed casket. Bach."

Lane could feel her mother's fantasy surround her, could almost hear the music swelling. She could also supply the details Rena Grace left out in her telling: the packed church, the whispered praise that threatened to drown out the music, Lane standing by the coffin, handkerchief to her mouth, whispering, "Mother, Oh, Mother."

"Mother. . ." Lane said into the telephone.

"The only thing I couldn't quite visualize is exactly what dress you'll be wearing. I went through all your clothes in my mind's eye and nothing you have is halfway suitable. That blue silk you wore to Hattie's would surely disgrace us all. For once I want your dress to be appropriate. Is that so much to ask?"

"Mother. . ." Lane's voice rose in frustration and aggravation.

"All right, all right, go eat your breakfast. I shouldn't bother you with my problems. I'll bear them alone."

Lane paused while she considered, then rejected, all the things she could say to her mother.

"Maurina Elaine, are you there?"

"Yes, Mother."

"I'll come by for you up at two and we'll go pick something out."

"Something in black, but not the kind of black that makes Maurina Elaine look so watered down. Sort of blue-black or even navy," Rena Grace said to the sales clerk. Rena Grace prided herself on being liberal about dress at funerals, allowing navy and forest green. "Maurina Elaine, what are you doing?"

Lane wound the silk scarf around her neck. "What do you think of this one, Mother?"

"We are not here to look at scarves, Maurina Elaine. Do come and sit down."

Lane lingered at the scarf counter twisting the silk until this small rebellion began to make her feel "nervous"—a word she used a great deal. She joined her mother on the beige pouf in the middle of the shop. Rena Grace took up most of the pouf with her girth, her hat, her bags and coat. She always called Bernaldo's to tell them when she was coming in to shop.

"I wish you would concentrate on what we are doing, Marina Elaine."

"And what *are* we doing?"

"You know very well, you exasperating child."

"I'm 47. And I'm not exasperating."

Yes, you are. You surely are." Silence. "I just want it all done right, Maurina Elaine."

"And I, of course, couldn't do it right?" Lane voice began to rise. "I can't do anything right."

"I'm simply trying to make things a little easier for you, Maurina Elaine, by planning out some of the details in advance." Rena Grace patted her daughter's hand. They sat quietly for a moment.

"Fashions may change in 20 years. What if the dress is out of style by the time you die?"

Rena Grace apparently hadn't considered this. "Well, I guess we'll just inspect it once a year. When I brush my funeral dress in the spring." She stored it in her closet in a box marked FUNERAL DRESS in black magic marker. She showed Lane where she kept it at least three times a year.

"For heaven's sake, Mother, you don't have to brush that dress every year. I'd see it was right before we went and buried you in it."

"Well, I know you. You might not pay attention to the cuffs the way you should. I just want to be sure."

Lane sighed heavily and pulled her hand away.

One by one the saleswomen in the small shop came up to say good afternoon to Miss Rena Grace, and to offer coffee and chocolate mint wafers. They spoke to Lane only as an afterthought, if at all.

Mrs. Carlson, the clerk who always waited on Rena Grace, and resembled her in body size and shape, held up four dark dresses. "Is this what you had in mind?"

"Not the wool. We want it for all seasons." Rena Grace surveyed the dresses critically. "Maybe the navy. Maybe the black with the shawl collar. Hm. I don't know about that other black. What do you think, Maurina Elaine?"

I think I'd like a scarf to go with my blue silk you hate so much.

"Maurina Elaine?"

"I like the navy."

"Well, try it on. And the black with the shawl collar."

The dresses didn't fit. The navy almost did.

"It's too short, don't you think, Mother?"

"You're just too tall. Your father's side of the family."

"We can take this hem down a full two inches." Mrs. Carlson inspected the underside of the dress as Lane stood between the mirror and her mother on the pouf.

Lane turned this way and that. There wasn't a mirror with a good light in her whole apartment, and she didn't realize just how *old* she looked.

"It makes you too thin." Rena Grace turned her head to the side, considering. "Turn around."

She buys a dress like she used to buy a horse, Lane realized, remembering stamping horseflesh being critically appraised. She felt sway-backed, lame, split-hoofed.

"No. It won't do. Try on the black again."

"Oh, Mother. You saw how that looked. They'd bury *me!*"

"True enough. Never seen such sallow skin. You got my sisters' names but not their complexions."

"There's this one." Mrs. Carlson produced the third dress, the one which Rena Grace finally bought, although Lane still liked the navy.

"We should have gotten the blue one," Lane told her mother on the way home, "I could've let it out."

You'd be tempted to wear it to church, then forget and cook dinner in it. Before long it'd be splotched and botched. You just don't have good sense about clothes, Maurina Elaine. Like that blue silk of yours."

"But, Mother, the blue silk is a good dress." You don't like it because you didn't pick it out yourself, Lane wanted to say, but didn't.

Lane remembered another scene in front of a mirror, her mother sighing and telling Lane how downright ugly she looked in a ruby red taffeta she'd wanted to wear to impress her date for the Junior-Senior high school prom, a football tackle her mother disapproved of. She'd ended up with a shell pink tucked batiste which Rena Grace claimed made her look "sweet." The football player spent most of the prom dancing with a cheerleader while Lane, in deep, wild misery, pretended to talk to her history teacher.

The tackle had been the first in a long line of suitors who didn't work out, but something large and bulky stood in the way of Lane seeing to the end of why. She just knew they were gone, that one by one they'd lost interest or been so severely criticized by Rena Grace that Lane couldn't bear to remain in the room with them. And now she looked so *old.*

"Besides, the deep black is really more suitable for a daughter," her mother continued. The very thought of deep black mourning made Rena Grace reach for a small, lace-trimmed handkerchief.

About a year later, Rena Grace devoted another of her morning calls to the dress. Lane let the phone ring 18 times before answering.

"I think it will do again for this year."

"Yes, I think so. I haven't worn it."

"Well, that's good news. Estelle"—Rena Grace's cook of 25 years—"said she'd never seen you in it."

"It doesn't fit."

"It fits fine. Don't start that again."

"Anyway, I've got to get ready for work."

"Work? Oh, you mean the library."

"I *work* at the library."

"We *had* the dress altered. They sent me quite a bill."

"Breakfast. I have to fix my breakfast."

"Why are you working on Saturday?"

"We all have to work on Saturday now. I told you."

"That's right. I'm finding it harder and harder to remember things these days."

"Mother, I've told you at least five times that if I want to be counted on as a full time staff member, I have to be willing to work Saturdays."

"Well, work part time again."

"I can't afford it since they raised my rent. I *told* you."

"As I say, I have a hard time remembering things."

Only things that don't have to do with you personally, Lane decided, stabbing at the yolks of her two eggs. "I need about $100 a month more than I make working part time." Lane hadn't given up hope that, for once, her mother would offer to help.

"You'll have plenty when I go, Maurina Elaine," Rena Grace answered complacently.

"But I need it now, Mother. Or I can't keep my apartment unless I work full time."

"But you have a lovely home here, Maurina Elaine, if you weren't too stubborn to move back. Your apartment's so small, you can't turn around twice. Can't move at all without falling over some stack of books or papers you keep lying around. I've got a whole houseful of room here. "

"Mother," Lane's voice had started to waver although they'd been over this ground time and time again since she'd moved out at 42, after the family doctor had tactfully suggested she might be less nervous if she lived alone. "I think it is best that I keep my own separate apartment. I can walk to the library, I can take care of my cat. It's just better all the way around."

"Well, keep your apartment." Rena Grace's voice rose higher and higher. "Forget how it looks to other people. Keep it, keep it."

"I intend to, Mother," Lane made one more stab at neutrality, "but that isn't the point. The issue is that from now on, I'll have to work every day plus every other Saturday which, believe it or not, you of great leisure and unlimited means," Lane was sobbing now, "takes away time and energy I don't always have."

"Surely a mother knows more than a doctor does about what's best for her own daughter. You belong at home."

"I *am* at home," Lane shouted into the phone before she hung up. "I'm 48 years old. I live here."

The next year, Rena Grace was on her trip to Italy and sent her daughter a card: "Italy is lovely but full of Italians. Have Bernaldo's take up your dress. Skirts in Europe very short this year. Love, Mother."

The year after that they added a black lace jabot, although Lane really wanted a white one. As the years passed, the hem came back down, then went up again, then down. When wide shoulders came in, they added thick pads which made Lane look so stylish Rena Grace seemed a little disappointed she didn't die while that fashion lasted.

The last spring, Rena Grace, who was having what they called"a good day" after a winter of bad ones, asked Lane to take her to Bernaldo's, and to call to say they were coming in.

"Greetings, Miss Rena Grace." Mrs. Carlson met them at the door. "It's so nice to see you again." The pouf had long since given way to an underwear counter, so they had to stand.

Lane, looking more and more faded herself, could tell that her mother didn't recognize Mrs. Carlson, but pretended to. "And you, my dear?" Rena Grace asked the stout woman, "How have you been?"—which happened to be the wrong thing to say to someone who'd recently had her gall bladder removed.

"I haven't been well, myself." Mrs. Carlson began with relish. "Not at all. Last fall I started having these pains. Just here. My husband rushed me to the doctor right away and he said that if I had them again, they'd have to take it out. My gall bladder. And you know, that's just what happened. Over Christmas. They told me not to eat rich foods, but they didn't tell me how to go about getting through the holidays without doing it. I mean, we went over to Annie's and she'd just made her first nut cake, so I took just a little bit not to hurt her feelings. Then Bill's wife made a whole tin of cheese wafers and I couldn't hurt *her* feelings. And that was just the beginning. I mean you can't be both polite and healthy. Not at Christmas. Mr. Carlson said to me, 'You're going to end up going under the knife if you aren't careful.' Got so, on top of everything else, I'd get indigestion from him warning me so much! When Annie made that nut cake, her first nut cake, Mr. Carlson said to me. . . "

Lane drifted off to look at the summer sweaters. They kept the library icy throughout the spring and summer. She hadn't had time to shop all year, her mother being so sick and all. She'd already tried on most of the sweaters from the rack when she heard her mother calling. "Maurina Elaine, we must leave. We mustn't keep Papa waiting."

Papa?

"Mother?" Lane took Rena Grace's arm and guided her towards the exit. Rena Grace seemed to come to herself a little.

"Goodbye, everyone."

"Goodbye, Miss Rena Grace, thank you for stopping by to see us." Mrs. Carlson, her broad face smooth and blank, walked with them to the door. "Take care of your mama, Lane."

On the sidewalk, Miss Rena Grace shook herself out as if she'd gotten covered with something unpleasant in the shop. "That woman talks so much! I don't know why Papa hired her."

"Papa?"

"Papa hired that woman before he died, so when he left me the store, I just had to keep her on."

"Mother," Lane began, "listen to me."

"No. I won't think of firing her now. Papa wouldn't have approved."

"You don't own the shop, Mother. Your father had a dry goods store. Maybe that's what you're thinking of?"

"It's family loyalty I'm thinking of. I'd never go against Papa's wishes." Rena Grace shook her head and the two vertical lines above her mouth deepened in disapproval. "I'm surprised at you, Maurina Elaine. And deeply hurt."

Lane could feel the old pain rise. "I'd better take you home."

"Don't you bother. One of my children will come and get me." "But, Mother, I *am* one of your children. I'm the only one left."

Rena Grace looked at her meanly. "My son Arthur is on his way."

"Arthur has been dead for 20 years. I will take you home." Rena Grace looked at her daughter blankly. "You don't even *see* me, do you Mother? Other people don't either. There's just a sort of a blank where a person should have been."

"Arthur will be here soon. My son Arthur will take me home."

"Well, did you ever!"

"Never."

Lane overheard them as she entered the crowded church and moved slowly down the aisle on the usher's arm.

"Rena Grace is going to jump right up out of her coffin." The old woman's whisper carried at least six pews.

Lane held a handkerchief to her mouth, pressing against a tide of unaccustomed emotion.

"Will you just look at that dress!"

Lane passed her aunts, Maurina and Elaine, from whom she'd gotten her names, but not her skin. She pretended to sag a little, slowing so she could hear their muttered whispers.

"To think Maurina Elaine would dress like that at her own mother's funeral."

"Blood red."

"Maurina Elaine never did have a lick of sense about clothes. Rena Grace said it a hundred times."

Lane's pressed the handkerchief harder to her mouth. Bach's music swelled as Lane stood with her hand on the closed casket, bowed her head and whispered, "Mother. Oh, Mother."

***

Postscript: After my sister read the story, she said that I'd gotten it all mixed up, that Laura had worn the dress to the funeral, but had gone to K-Mart and bought the tackiest sweater she could find and worn it over the dress.

Kimberley Snow

EXERCISE

1. Expand and develop a short story you wrote as one of the previous exercises. Experiment turning it (or parts of it) into a play.

WRITING WORKSHOPS

A writing workshop can be very useful in providing deadlines, feedback, and a sense of not being alone. You can join a workshop simply for the pleasure of getting together with others to share ideas and writings. Or you can let the workshop function as a sort of way-station towards publication: a place where you present a piece to a small, knowledgeable (usually sympathetic) circle, then refine and rewrite it before going public. Or both.

If you want to start a workshop, put a notice up on a bulletin board of your local women's center, community college, or bookstore. Suggest a time and place to meet, then let the group decide on the ongoing structure in the first meeting.

The exercises in WORD PLAY/WORD POWER provide a quick way for a group to get started, assuming not everyone has a work in progress. During the first meeting, you may want to write as a group, then share your work. On subsequent meetings, bring in xeroxed copies of exercises or other work completed at home. Let these exercises evolve into stories, poems, essays, which you continue to rewrite and refine in light of the group's feedback. It helps to keep a workshop small (about three to five working members is plenty). In a larger group, especially if each member writes a great deal, there is the problem of covering everyone's work in any sort of depth. How often you meet depends on you. Some groups meet weekly for six weeks, then never again. Others have been meeting once a month for years. The group that I'm in used to meet once a month, but now meets only when someone finishes a project and wants feedback on it. In general, all workshops are defined by time available, work produced, and the quality of the group's interaction.

Before asking a new member to join a group, it is a good idea to have this writer to come as a guest for several meetings. Try to find writers who are at about the same level of expertise and ambition. Avoid people who are highly defensive, excessively negative, or narcissistic.

The writing workshops that I've been in work this way: each member brings in a portion of a work in progress, hands out xeroxed copies to the group, then reads aloud. The members of the group then "workshop" the piece: How does it function as a whole? Do all the parts fit together? How can it be improved? Is the voice right? Is it clear? What succeeds best in the piece? What are its strengths? An honest but non-judgmental approach is always best when giving critiques in a workshop setting.

The stress in your workshop may not be on writing at all, but on the issues raised by the exercises, as in a consciousness raising group. Or you might want to use WORD PLAY/WORD POWER as the basis of a reading group, using the writing exercises as a springboard for discussion. But writing together and/

or sharing what you've written creates a unique atmosphere. Offering your own words to others and responding to theirs is a form of generosity which can create a common bond as well as an appreciation of another's methods and techniques.

SUGGESTED RESOURCES

There are many good books about writing on the market. The following are especially helpful:

Dorothea Brande. BECOMING A WRITER. New York: Houghton-Mifflin, 1981. Reprint of a 1934 self-help book filled with practical and detailed suggestions on writing.

Rita Mae Brown. STARTING FROM SCRATCH. New York, Bantam, 1988. An interesting, readable, useful, inspiring book with a nuts-and-bolts approach.

Natalie Goldberg. WRITING DOWN THE BONES: Freeing the Writer Within. Boston: Shambhala, 1986. Using Zen techniques, Goldberg teaches writers how to "unlearn" wrong-headed assumptions about composition and tap into their creativity. Unusual and energizing.

Peter Elbow. WRITING WITH POWER. Oxford: Oxford University Press, 1981. Practical techniques for mastering the writing process.

Peter Elbow. WRITING WITHOUT TEACHERS. New York: Oxford University Press, 1973. Excellent common sense approach. Very helpful chapters on free writing and setting up and working in writing groups.

Joanna Field. A LIFE OF ONE'S OWN. Los Angeles, J.P. Tarcher, Inc., 1981. Originally printed in 1936, this book chronicles a journey of self-exploration via diary and journal into awareness and authenticity. Fields is also the author of two other books which deal with creativity: AN EXPERIMENT IN LEISURE and ON NOT BEING ABLE TO PAINT.

Daniel D. Pearlman and Paula R. Pearlman. GUIDE TO RAPID REVISION. Indianapolis: Bobbs-Merrill Educational Publishing, 1982. A quick and easy guide for grammar rules and correct usage. Leaves out the things you don't need to know.

Gabriele Lussar Rico. WRITING THE NATURAL WAY: Using Right-Brain Techniques to Release Your Expressive Power. Los Angeles: J. P. Tarcher, Inc., 1983. Stresses enhancing creativity and writing confidence by using such techniques as clustering and visualization.

Wm. Strunk, Jr. and E.B. White. ELEMENTS OF STYLE. New York: Macmillan, 1979. A lean classic with clear cut rules about style and usage.

Brenda Ueland. IF YOU WANT TO WRITE: A Book about Art, Independence and Spirit. Saint Paul: Graywolf Press, 1987. First published in 1938, this excellent book by a remarkable woman includes such chapters as "Why You Are Not to Be Discouraged, Annihilated by Rejection Slips," and "Why Women Who do too Much Housework Should Neglect it for their Writing."

William Zinsser. ON WRITING WELL. New York: Harper & Row, 1980. Informal guide to writing good non-fiction.

MARKETING YOUR WORK

If you wish to try to market your writing, the bookstore has a shelf of books to tell you how to write and sell everything from erotica to children's books, from young adult to science fiction. They usually make it sound easy and fun. It isn't. Often it takes months just to get a manuscript read by a publisher before he rejects it and then you've got to start all over again. Often this same manuscript has been edited and rewritten and restructured 12 or 13 times before you even began to send it out. Frustration lurks behind every corner when you try to become a professional writer, rejection dogs you like a spaniel.

Even though the publishing guides tend to minimize the down side of the process, these books can be helpful for the novice writer. The following give you the names and addresses of editors and publishers, plus useful guidelines for submitting your work:

1989 FICTION WRITER'S MARKET. Writer's Digest Books, Cincinnati, Ohio.

1989 POET'S MARKET: Where and How To Publish Your Poetry, Writer's Digest Books, Cincinnati, Ohio.

THE WRITER'S HANDBOOK. Edited by Sylvia Burack. The Writer, Inc. Boston, MA.

1989 WRITER'S MARKET: Where to Sell What You Write, Writer's Digest Books, Cincinnati, Ohio.

In addition, your reference librarian can help you find other writer's guides which are also published yearly. If you are trying to market a novel, you will want to look at the guides to literary agents that are available. Virtually no major publishing house will take an unagented manuscript these days and getting an agent is almost as hard as getting a publisher. So it is time well spent to read up on how to get an agent.

If you are primarily interested in publishing short fiction or poetry, however, it is still possible to proceed without an agent. Addresses of magazines and journals that publish poetry or short stories may be found in the journals themselves. But when first starting out, it is best to use the writer's guides mentioned above for they give such information as what type of story a magazine prefers, how many poems a journal publishes in an issue, and whether or not the magazine pays anything. Usually for poetry, they do not, but some journals will give you several copies of the issue in which you appear. With short stories, it depends on the publication—but don't expect to get rich.

The general procedure is to send out one short story or a set of poems: three or four short ones, one or two long ones. Editors don't want to be inundated with a closetful of work (and you don't want to have to pay the postage back and forth on huge piles of manuscript pages). Each submission should be neatly typed of course, with your name and address in the upper left hand corner. Always keep a copy of what you send out, or submit a good, clean copy and keep the original. Always enclose a self addressed stamped envelope (SASE). If you don't do this, you won't get anything back.

A short note should accompany your submission. It should be addressed to the current appropriate editor. (The above guides will give you their names or call the main office number and ask if Joe Poem is still the poetry editor-- but do not request to actually speak to him. If you manage to get through you'll be on the outs forever for bothering him.) Keep your letter simple and to the point. Always avoid wordiness, apology, cuteness, flattery, and vagueness. Just something such as: "I am submitting the enclosed poems for your consideration." If you've been published elsewhere, be sure to include that.

Allow six weeks to a year for a reply. Resist the impulse to call and find out what's happening to your work. Editors *hate* to be called by eager would-be authors. I've had editors tell me they've instantly thrown in the trash work by anyone who bugs them. It is true that the Post Office does lose mail so if you're the nervous type, send it return receipt requested and resist the impulse to phone.

Often a journal will keep your work for eight months (or longer), then return it with a printed rejection slip—or without a single comment. Do not take this personally or as a reflection on the quality of your work. Editors are overworked, underpaid, and sometimes have very eccentric taste.

Keep a record of where you have submitted what. An easy method is simply to write the name of the journal and the date in the upper right hand corner of your duplicate copy, then cross it off when the poem or story comes back, and write the next date and place of submission underneath it. With this method you can tell at a glance who you have sent it to and when. Most poems and stories that find their way into print have been submitted several times. A widely published poet in Santa Barbara claims that his record for sending a single poem out is 52 times.

When your work comes back from an editor, look it over, rewrite it if it seems to need it, then send it out again. Everyone will tell you not to multiple submit your work (send out the same piece to several different editors), but many people do this. "They don't care about me, so why should I care about them?" a poet friend once explained. The problem, of course, is that if the same story is accepted in two different places, you have to withdraw it from one of them: they get mad, and never publish you again.

At first, after nothing but rejection slips, a hand scrawled note on the printed slip begins to seem like a success. Such words as "try us again" or "nice poem, but not for us" or—and this one is a killer—"we almost took this one" come to mean a great deal. An editor who will take the time to actually criticize your work is a blessing.

Then (hopefully) comes the happy day when your SASE is returned but seems a little light. A note from the editor tells you that your work has been accepted! The rejection slips and the endless waiting are forgotten, you are going to be a published writer!

NOTE TO TEACHERS

This book is designed to be able to be used in writing or in women's studies classes, alone or in conjunction with other texts. Some of the exercises can form the basis of class discussion, others work best if written out, still others are more suitable for private, personal work than for the classroom.

When I first started using writing assignments in women's studies classes, I had students write at home and keep a notebook of all the exercises they completed to be handed in at the end of the term. In time, I found it more workable for students to hand in five to ten of their best exercises—rewritten and typed. As an alternative, some students chose to expand and polish a single short story, set of poems, or a brief play that grew out of one of the exercises.

I eventually discovered that it also works well in women's studies classes occasionally to assign an exercise (or a related group of exercises, such as the ones on gender), have students write in class for about 20 minutes, then open the topic for class discussion. In non-writing classes, I don't ask the students to read what they've just written, but simply to talk about what they learned as they wrote. Since writing stirs up ideas and emotions that normally stay submerged, these discussions can become quite lively.

In a class where a number of students elect to turn in a creative writing project rather than a term paper, I try to set aside a day or two towards the end of the term when the students read their short stories or poems to the class. Depending on the number (and talent) of students and the xerox allowance, the teacher might also reproduce one or more of the better student papers, even create a short anthology.

In writing classes there is generally more time for in-class writings and small group discussions than in women's studies courses. Many students find that when they are first asked to write in class, they are unable to do so effectively, but by the end of the term they've come to rely on the group process. Depending on the length and type of writing class, I usually set aside 20 minutes of each class period for in-class writing.

Naturally, in writing classes, there is more stress on the finished product. In these classes, certain exercises (WRITING FOR PLEASURE, for instance) are used for warm-up or pre-writing only, not to be turned in or graded. I've found that while some students enjoy reading what they've written in class, others are quite shy. Breaking down into small groups after doing an in-class writing exercise provides a semi-workshop atmosphere that can be quite stimulating to sharing—and learning—even among the more timid.

Small groups can, of course, be invaluable to a writing class. (As we all know, they can also be a complete waste of time.) Usually, a group of four or five seems to works best. Ideally, each person reads all or part of the exercise just completed, then others give constructive feedback as to the content and the writing. Rewritten versions can be submitted to the same group in the next round. This structure tends to work best in advanced writing seminars.

The writing exercises in WORD PLAY/WORD POWER are many and wide ranging, and may be modified in various ways. As I pointed out in USING THIS BOOK, they may be adapted and combined, shortened or lengthened, expanded or contracted to suit a particular classroom.

SUBJECT INDEX

NOTE TO READERS/WRITERS

If you wish to share your writing, please send a xeroxed copy of an exercise (or exercises) to me at this address:

Conari Press
713 Euclid Ave.
Berkeley, CA 94708

Future editions of WORD PLAY/WORD POWER may include reader/ writer samples of some of the exercises. Sending in your sample (sorry, it cannot be returned) constitutes permission to use it. If you wish to remain anonymous, please indicate so; otherwise your name and hometown will be used.

ABOUT THE AUTHOR

Kimberley Snow, Ph.D. is a teacher of writing and women's studies at the University of California, Santa Barbara. A prize-winning playwright, she is also the author of two novels, a cookbook, and numerous reviews and articles.